Born in 1962, Colin Fry received his first message at the age of ten and became a professional medium at seventeen. He has toured internationally and has his own television show, *6ixth Sense*, on Living TV. One of the leading lights in the psychic mediumship world, Colin uses his spiritual knowledge to offer life-changing advice and support to people, providing sensible down-to-earth explanations about the strange world of the paranormal and supernatural. He is the author of *Life Before Death*.

By the same author:

Life Before Death

Secrets From the Afterlife

Colin Fry

LONDON · SYDNEY · AUCKLAND · JOHANNESBURG

9 10

First published in Great Britain in 2008 by Rider,
an imprint of Ebury Publishing
A Random House Group Company

The Random House Group Limited Reg. No. 954009

Addresses for companies within the Random House Group can be found at
www.rbooks.co.uk

A CIP catalogue record for this book is available from the British Library

The Random House Group Limited supports The Forest Stewardship
Council (FSC), the leading international forest certification organisation.
All our titles that are printed on Greenpeace approved FSC certified paper
carry the FSC logo. Our paper procurement policy can be found at
www.rbooks.co.uk/environment

Printed and bound in Great Britain by
CPI Cox & Wyman, Reading, RG1 8EX

ISBN 978-1-84-604092-4

To buy books by your favourite authors and register for offers visit
www.rbooks.co.uk

The author would like to thank Thorsons and HarperCollins for permission
to quote material from *A Return to Love* by Marianne Williamson (1996).

*The stories in this book are based upon real events, but names and some details
have been changed to protect the privacy of those involved.*

This book is dedicated to my niece Kimberley,
who I believe will always reach for the stars.

With much love,
Uncle Colin

Contents

Introduction

I 'VE been able to communicate with the spirit world since I was ten years old. By communicating I mean that sometimes I see a person or a picture, other times I might hear a voice. Often I just get an overwhelming, powerful sense that I'm in the presence of someone who has passed over. I never know how a spirit will come to me but I do know my role and purpose in this scenario is to tune in, to get on the same wavelength, sense the messages and to try to understand and interpret them. Today my gift is to see, feel, listen and talk with spirits. For me this form of communication is an amazing, life-affirming event. It reminds me over and over again that we are not humans having a spiritual experience: we are spirits having a human experience which we share with others. It also reassures me that there is more to our existence than this earthly life; that there is an afterlife.

I am often asked by people what the afterlife is. In fact, this is a question that has perplexed mankind since the dawn of time. Throughout history, great minds have tried to fathom whether there is another level of existence after our earthly life has come to an end and, if so, what its nature must be like. Some have claimed that the good and deserving will be rewarded with a tranquil paradise when they have passed over, whereas pain and anguished purgatory await wrongdoers. More compassionate theories such as those of reincarnation provide second, third and even fourth opportunities for us to take earthly form in a bid to get it right, eventually earning our place in paradise! You might be surprised to learn that even amongst mediums and psychics descriptions of the afterlife and its environments vary, which only adds to the vast majority of people's confusion over the matter.

My own communications with the spirit world have taught me that the afterlife is a very personal experience. I'm unable to offer you an absolute definition of it as I don't possess the gift to see into eternity any more than anyone else does. And, even if I could, I would be reluctant to offer you a fixed definition of the afterlife, as I have found that when we are set in our views and ways we close the door to growth. However, I will say this much: every concept of the afterlife is highly individual, whether it entails a paradise, a hell or a purgatory. It would seem that in the afterlife we are greeted by many possibilities, which in my opinion is summed up perfectly in the Bible by the words 'in my Father's house there are many mansions'. Initially, we all seem to experience the results of our beliefs.

This means that if we approach the afterlife with hope in our hearts then we are more likely to visualise a heavenly paradise when we get there. For some of us, this paradise may be inspired by religious teaching and we may believe we will obtain heaven through our obedience to a particular spiritual moral code. But it's worth remembering that strict spiritual moral codes can be misinterpreted and lead to terrible earthly atrocities committed in the name of religion. Similarly, it seems that those who approach the afterlife with fear in their souls experience dark visions of Dante-like infernos; they dwell on the sinful moments in their lives and are afraid that those single moments of error have condemned their souls to eternal suffering – another example of a harmful, set way of thinking.

There was a time when I used to get very irritated when I heard certain mediums and spiritual types waffle on about the afterlife as though it were some sort of rose-tinted paradise; their portrayals of it seemed all a bit too romantic to be true and in my view seemed to bear more resemblance to Disneyland than heaven! However, having given the matter more thought over the years, and having considered carefully my own mediumistic visions of life beyond earthly existence, I now realise that if we condition ourselves to expect an afterlife of fluffy clouds then of course that is precisely what we will initially experience when we pass over. By the same token, if we have taken no pleasure in life or harboured negative attitudes towards others, no doubt we will discover that our afterlife is initially bleak and sad.

A few years ago I sat down to watch a film with some friends called *When Dreams May Come*, starring Robin Williams. The film is about a man and his wife who tragically lose their children. Then the character played by Robin Williams is killed, leaving behind his distraught wife who goes on to take her own life. It was not so much the plot of the film that impressed me (although I do think it's a very good film); it was the representation of the afterlife that really struck me as being the nearest to what I as a medium have personally experienced. In the film, the individual members of the family initially found themselves in environments in the afterlife that were appropriate to their earthly life, experiences and behaviour. They each had work to be completed on their own before they were finally brought together.

The film also showed how the afterlife is not a meaningless meandering through eternity, but a process in which individual souls seek out and are of service to other souls, both discarnate and incarnate. For me, this idea helps us to have a clearer understanding of what people mean when they talk about guardian angels and spirit guides. The role of these spirits seems to be to inspire and guide us towards harmony and a positive life that is creative, rather than chaotic disharmony and destructive negativity.

From my experience, it seems that illness and disease do not exist in the afterlife as the spirit form is incorruptible. However, as microscopic life-forms such as viruses and bacteria – both essential parts of creation – also have to die, then it is possible that the energy of such things performs other functions in the fabric of the ether of the afterlife. On that note, it once occurred to me that history is filled with myths and legends about magical creatures such as unicorns, griffins and mermaids, and that these creatures might have been originally inspired by visions of extinct life-forms that once dwelled on the earth, but which later appeared in disincarnate beautified spirit form! But that is just a personal theory.

Several years ago, when I was the owner of a college in Sweden, I walked in on a group of students who were having a very animated conversation about angels. They were discussing whether angels had wings or not; half of them were convinced they had, whereas the other half thought not. They wanted to know my opinion. I explained that I believed our minds can only comprehend the intangibility of spirit existence and the afterlife according to our individual experiences, expectations and beliefs. Does that make what we experience with respect to angels and the afterlife any less real? No, of course not – if our minds will only accept the biblical depiction of winged angels then that's precisely what we will see if we encounter one; however, if our understanding of angels is different then we will naturally be open to a broader perception of angelic forms.

In order for us to settle down and embrace our eternal existence when we pass over, the afterlife has to take the form of something that appears comfortable and acceptable to our awareness when we first leave this mortal life. So it might at first seem that the afterlife is nothing more than a state of mind. This may be an unsettling idea to come to terms with when we have been used to judging reality through hard evidence and facts. In life, we are often reliant on what we experience through our five senses of hearing, sight, smell, taste and touch. We make sense of our place in the world through the things around us that we can react to. However, what if I were to tell you that we might even create this world through the power of our thoughts? This being so, why should we fear an afterlife that is less dense than this earthly existence; that is not governed by the laws of time, space, matter and physical form, and that responds to the power of our thoughts?

There is one thing I feel I can say for sure: our conduct and how we interact with each other while we are on this earthly plane seem to form the building blocks of the environment we initially experience when we leave the physical world. This means that we would do well to think carefully about how we behave and connect with each other in this earthly life as we are all part of a bigger picture.

Throughout the ages people have told stories as a way of making sense of the world we live in, as well as a way of sharing and bringing people together. You will know many stories yourself – they might be tales from your grandparents that you heard sitting at their knee, stories you heard huddled around a campfire, stories you have read or stories you once heard. Though we may not always realise it, much of what we know comes from these stories. Within them we can find many secrets that can help us to live our lives.

However, secrets don't only have to come from the here and now. They can also be directly offered to those of us who are able to make contact with loved ones who have passed over. These loved ones can be just as wise as anybody else here on this earth, and often more so because of their experience not only here but also on the spirit side of life.

The more I'm in touch with the spirit world the more I realise that the answers that so many people are looking for are already right in front of us: it's just that we need to be reminded of them. Those who have passed over can remind us that we have a duty to carry on, to look inside ourselves and to lead lives that are spiritually enriching. But the best part is, we don't need to leave this physical life to discover the secrets from the afterlife. By connecting with loved ones who have passed over we can come closer to them and also closer to what our own lives mean to us here and now. The closer we come to the truth of our lives and those of our loved ones, the less chance we have of repeating past mistakes.

This book shares some of the many secrets I have been privileged to learn in my readings and sittings over the years. They cover a variety of things, including the importance of love and friendship, hope, forgiveness, letting go and moving on. I hope that you will find them as helpful and inspiring as I have.

Colin Fry

1 | Secrets of Love and Friendship

Love is the most precious gift life has to offer us. It comes in many forms and has many levels of intensity. However, in my experience many of us fall in love with the idea of love. The fact is that we tend to project our ideal relationships onto our lives and, when that ideal doesn't become reality, we get upset and think, 'Oh no, it's all spoiled!'

I have a friend who found the first years of her marriage particularly difficult. Despite the fact that she and her husband were a wonderful match she couldn't cope when they fell out over little things.

I remember when she rang me once in tears, sobbing, 'My marriage is over!' It was all very dramatic.

'Why? I asked.

'We had an argument…' she sniffed.

Now how silly was that? Arguments are a necessary part of any relationship. However, a lot of what is written about love and friendships, and reflected in movies, TV, novels, popular songs, has nothing to do with what relationships are really about. Instead, it's a total fantasy.

At the time of writing this I am rapidly approaching forty-six years of age and I would happily admit that the past six years have been a great experience for me, as I've been in a very happy relationship with my partner for three years. But relationships are strange affairs. I won't pretend that all is sunshine and roses in the Fry home. Like every other couple in the world we irritate one another at times and endure the stresses of life together with all its hurdles, large and small. However, we respect and value the fact that we are able to offer one another so much in terms of companionship and love. This is why we don't allow the past to upset our present happiness: my partner and I both believe in behaving towards the exes in our lives in a civil manner. In my view, asking a partner to banish their past is wrong and only shows a weakness in your own faith in the partnership you have.

These days, we have an added dimension to our relationship in that my line of work is not what you might call 'normal'! After I've been away on a long tour or out filming, we have to renew our relationship: take a few days to get it back to some sort of equilibrium and make time for each other. The American novelist Tom Robbins once said, 'We waste time looking for the perfect lover, instead of creating the perfect love.' Love takes effort and things don't always go to plan in relationships, but that is life – as this story from my own family demonstrates.

My Great Uncle Charles

I had a great uncle called Charles who was a marvellous, wonderful man. He was an interesting character who didn't have an easy life. When he was little, he'd been packed off into a children's home along with my grandma and her siblings after my great grandma tragically committed suicide at the age of thirty-two.

Time passed and the boys in the family all became young soldiers. Charles himself joined the Military Band and then went on to play in the wind section for Bournemouth Symphony Orchestra, becoming a very accomplished player. But at the height of his career he was struck down with Parkinson's disease. This meant huge changes not just to his own life but also to that of Vera, his wonderful wife. No longer just his loving partner, my great aunt was now also his carer and nursemaid. This man she loved was now her patient. And the tragedy was that she knew – as did he – that he would never get well again.

This was a sad episode in an already poignant love story. These two had not been married very long when my great uncle fell ill. And to make matters worse, they'd had to wait to get married in the first place because, although they had fallen in love, Charles's first wife had refused to grant him a divorce. For my great aunt Vera there was always a sense she and Charles were playing catch up with each other; that they didn't have the life they should have had because of circumstances. She felt that she wasn't getting enough of her Charles and I can imagine that when the

Parkinson's was diagnosed she probably thought, 'I haven't had him with me long and now he's being taken away!' Nobody could deny it was very hard for them both. In the end, the illness was with him a long time and he didn't pass over until he was well into his eighties.

Afterwards Vera naturally went through a period of feeling that she'd been cheated out of her great love. It wasn't supposed to be like that when you loved someone, was it? You were meant to have a blissful, happy life together, especially when you'd taken so long to find each other. In the end her broken heart was just too much and she made an impetuous decision to go to Canada so she could get away from it all. Very sadly, while she was there she developed Alzheimer's and eventually died.

Some time later I ran a psychic workshop. At it, a psychic artist drew a picture of my great uncle and aunt side by side. It was incredible since she had absolutely no idea who she was drawing, but it was clearly them. I rarely give messages from the afterlife to my own family but this time I showed the picture to my mum. She looked at it thoughtfully and then asked me what I thought it meant.

I considered it for a moment. 'You know, Mum,' I said, 'I think it means that Vera and Charles are happy together in the afterlife. I think they're saying no matter that their love didn't lead to the future that they'd hoped or planned for, it was still love and at least they had that time together.'

And their love was no less precious for that reason. Life had given Charles and Vera every reason for resentment and bitterness but their story tells us that we need to accept there is no perfect love or life.

Secret: our relationships may not always be perfect but we can treasure what we have.

I've often found – both personally and in my work – that the death of a relative can be a path for reunion, even reconciliation, among surviving relatives. (But at the other extreme, it can also tear families apart, especially in the case of sudden or violent death, so it's important to be sensitive to one another's approach to grief and to make sure we don't try and blame anyone.) Sharing a loss can make the burden of grief easier to carry: just having people there even if you have nothing particular to say gives you strength. At the same time you can think and talk about the person who's passed over and that can help you recover. It's all about creating a sense of community and it's something I very much believe in.

A Gathering

'OK, all right, come on then my love.'

I had a lady trying to connect to me but I seemed to be lost in the 1970s. I was actually seeing the television programme *House Party* as well as the image of a group of ladies who looked as though they were having quite a good time together. It seemed so strange, but it would make sense to the girl in front of me.

I smiled at her. 'Sally, this message is for you,' I confirmed. 'I believe this is your sister and your mum.'

Sally nodded. 'As soon as you mentioned *House Party*, I knew the message was for me.'

'OK,' I continued. 'I've got this lady connecting with me and she's showing me this little gathering of women and it reminds me of *House Party*. You know – a group of women who get together and put the world to rights. Oh, bless you – and she's saying, "I sort of miss that! I sort of miss that." She's saying it would be so nice if it could happen just one more time.'

Sally made a comment to the effect that there were not many of them left now.

'You mean the get-togethers are a bit thin on the ground now. Don't you do it anymore?'

'Yes,' she said wistfully.

I explained, 'For those of us that are in this physical life – and of course those that have passed – they're still possible. She's wondering why you don't do it.

'Now hang on a minute. She's telling me something. What are you talking about? Why are you laughing – come on! All right my love, I understand it now.' I looked directly into Sally's eyes. 'She was at first trying to be discreet, and she's now being very blunt about it: who's got the vein problem in their leg? Ah, my love, would you understand that you do know someone that you can borrow a support stocking from?! She's trying to be incredibly discreet to start with, hoping the penny will drop for you, and she's saying, "It's not going to drop; you're going to have to spell it out!"'

'Hmm, well she had a bad leg,' mumbled Sally. 'I suppose I've inherited it.'

'All right, either you've got to borrow it off someone or there's a compression band or compression stocking or compression sock involved, but she was trying to be incredibly discreet about it. Four nights ago you must have complained or thought about the fact that your leg was aching.'

'Gosh, that's spot on.' Sally looked stunned. 'I was talking to my girlfriends about having the vein done, asking them what they thought.'

'Ah right, OK.'

'It's interesting she's said that the subject hadn't come up at all before,' Sally said, a little bit puzzled.

'Well, my love,' I continued, 'she's taking me back four nights ago, and she's saying that you were either thinking about it very strongly or you were saying how much your leg was aching.'

Sally nodded in agreement. 'It's a bit of a family problem, the vein thing. I found out that Mum actually had a bad leg with varicose veins, and now I've developed a varicose vein too. That's why the subject of going in to hospital to have it stripped came up.'

'She's also speaking to me of disruption in the family over the recent passing of a loved one – but not herself,' I said, trying not to stir up recent painful memories.

'We lost a sister last year,' Sally replied sadly.

'Now your mum's referring to a card that expressed your sorrow and hope perfectly. Yes, it's definitely some sort of greeting card. You know what she means.'

'It was the card at my sister's funeral, saying that we hoped that she was going to be with my mum, because that's all she ever used to say is "I'm going to be with Mum", and that's all we ever wanted to know. And I know now that she's with my mum.'

Sally explained that the gatherings I had mentioned earlier had meant a lot to the women in the family: 'On a Thursday my sister used to come down from Surbiton, and we all used to get together, my other two sisters and my mum. We used to go round to Mum's, organise food and drink, and then we'd play cards, talk about things and enjoy ourselves and have a good time. My mum was a very caring person; I mean she brought six children up on her own, but she didn't only care for us, she cared for everybody. She took on everyone's problems and she would do anything for anybody.'

I passed on her mother's final message: 'She's saying you know it would be so nice, love, if it could happen just one more time.'

'Colin, I'll try to make sure it does after hearing this,' Sally said thoughtfully. 'I mean, I think she wants the three of us – me and my sisters – to get together one last time before one of my sisters moves to Hastings. I realise how important it is to share things and we haven't been doing that enough lately.' Sally brought her hand firmly down onto the arm of the sofa. 'I'm going to fix that,' she said resolutely. 'And I'm sure Mum and my sister will be there with us,' she added.

Secret: we should not give up our usual activities when loved ones have passed over. They are always there to share them with us.

I truly believe that love must be given without boundaries, otherwise it cannot flourish. I know I'm a very demonstrative person and affectionate with those whom I love. Aside from the fact that this has brought a tide of untold, wonderful, happiness to my life, I could be no other way. I enjoy giving generously to those who I'm close to. At the same time I'm also careful to give others room to breathe and grow. At least, I hope they see it that way too.

I think my outlook and desire to be of service to others comes from being mentored by older friends when I was younger. It was especially valuable and important to me because I was struggling in a world that is far less accepting than it is now. To have friends who were there to help me and advise me was a lifesaver. Now the mantle of mentor has passed to me and there is nothing I like better than to think I have helped someone on their way. For me this is part of my life's purpose and I get a genuine buzz out of guiding and advising others as people have done for me in my own life. Knowledge and experience are both gifts that we are not meant to keep to ourselves, but which should be passed on to others.

At the same time I know there is a difference between being helpful and being interfering. We all have to be careful that the strength of our friendships or relationships doesn't turn into possessiveness. We need to keep our relationships open to growth and change, happy to see those we care for flourish, and also be there to pick up the pieces when things go wrong. If a time comes when, either by death or changed circumstances, our path separates for a while from that of one we love, we should have faith that love will ensure that we will come together again, each of us having grown in the process – if not on this side of life, then probably on the other!

Sometimes we may find that, with the guidance and encouragement of others – even those in the afterlife – we are able to re-evaluate our relationships and to make a fresh start. The saying is that we choose our friends but we can't choose our family; however, we can certainly choose how we behave towards our kith and kin.

Brothers Apart

I stood in the studio on an absolutely gorgeous September day wondering if the weather would still be lovely when we finished later. The drive in had been glorious and it seemed that the sudden emergence of an Indian summer that week had put everyone in a positive mood. Perhaps that was why I was sure we would have some strong communications and, as it turned out, I was right. Now, I could feel another one coming through, a gentleman this time.

'OK, I'm over here somewhere.' I waved my hand over in the far-left direction of the audience. I stopped and got my bearings again. 'Hold on a minute, I feel an ark of light going over the four of you here together today.'

A man with a very deep, mellow voice spoke up. 'No, there're two of us.'

'Just the two of you, OK. What're your names?'

'Simon,' said the first man.

'Johnny,' snorted the second, as though he was amused to be singled out.

Even though they were both adults these two fellows looked cheeky and you could just tell they'd got up to no good in the past. I looked at Simon first. 'Sir, please would you be able to understand a gentleman who went to the spirit, who was not in the army but was in the Home Guard?'

The first man appeared to be totally puzzled and shook his head. 'No.'

I looked at the second man: 'How about you, sir, do you know who I might be referring to?'

Now the second man was staring at me, rapt. 'Yes, I know someone who was in the Home Guard.'

'All right, this is quite peculiar, what's going on here, because I've realised that I've got more than one person trying to connect to me. I've got the feeling that it's to do with both of you. Would you understand about someone who fell in or got thrown into a pond?'

The first man nodded in the affirmative. I turned to the second one. 'And you, sir?'

'No, but I threw someone in!' said Johnny.

'You threw someone in! Now why does that not surprise me, sir?' I smiled. The man raised his eyebrows and smiled back to acknowledge my remark.

I continued: 'Would you also understand about playing chicken with somebody with a dart?'

'A cross bow!' exclaimed Simon. 'Yes. When we were seventeen or eighteen we were having a few drinks, me and a few friends up at the flat that we rented at the time, and what we decided to do – sounds stupid now – was put a cross bow and apple on somebody's head and try with the cross bow to see who could hit it! Then we'd play chicken with a cross bow and an apple on somebody's head! Lucky for both of us, we weren't very good shots and it just went through the wall, basically.'

'All right – you understand the connection to Peter?'

Simon responded once more but this time he pointed to Johnny. 'He's got a brother, Peter.'

'Right, so Peter's *your* brother,' I turned to Johnny. 'I'll come back to you in a minute then.' Then I said, 'And there were the group of kids who hung around the chapel, or it could be Chapel Road or Chapel Street.'

Johnny said he couldn't remember exactly where but that there were 'loads of them' who hung around together in the Chapel Road area.

'What's this about getting chased out of a cemetery?' I wondered.

Simon pointed to Johnny once more. 'That'll be him again.'

I turned to Johnny who just shrugged and said, 'Yep'. The audience laughed.

'All right, now I understand. And in this cemetery there was a small building or a chapel?'

'Yes. We used to catch people coming out of the cemetery, then tie them to crosses (they were normally friends of ours!) and then go to the pub and have a few drinks before we'd let them go – except sometimes we forgot because we were too drunk!' confessed Johnny.

'Ah, thank you, because he's saying, "They didn't think I knew about these things, but tell them I do." We must be going back to the early 1970s now. I also want this thing about "four" clarified. Four lads who all went round together, and if it wasn't the parkas it was the crombie jackets?'

'That was me,' said Simon.

'OK, so who flushed Peter's head down a toilet?'

This time Johnny admitted it was him.

'And Peter isn't younger than you,' I added.

'No, older.'

'So why did you bully him and mess about with his books?'

'Because I was tough with him.'

'Right, OK, the feeling that I'm getting from your

grandad is that you're a lovable rogue. That's what he says.'

'Oh, thanks Grandad!' said Johnny sarcastically.

I let that go and noted, 'Your grandad was always quite fond of you. He thought you could do absolutely no wrong.'

'Which as you can see, Colin, is quite right of course!' Johnny gave a little snigger. There were giggles again from the audience.

'All right, your grandad is just asking me to tell you to give Peter a bit of your time. Do you comprehend what he's saying here?'

'Yes, I understand that.'

'And he's just saying, "Son, stop trying to toughen the boy up, he can't be you. Just let him be himself and respect and appreciate him for that." Do you understand that?'

Johnny looked distinctly sheepish. 'Yes, I know what he's saying. The thing is, I don't see much of my brother to be quite honest, and as for what he said about the books it was him: my brother always used to read books all the time. I must admit I've neglected him a bit recently. He rings me up quite a lot but I don't bother ringing him back. I just feel I have nothing in common with him so I don't see the point in us chatting. I must ring him, that's what my grandad's saying.'

'Yes, but I think he also wants you to actually try to show a bit of interest?'

'I suppose I could do that,' Johnny said reluctantly.

I continued: 'He says you might not understand it but

you should show a bit of interest. Just a little. It will make a big difference to your brother.'

Johnny wriggled in his seat as though he was suddenly a little bit ashamed of the way he had behaved in the past. I had a feeling that when he left the studio that day his relationship with his brother might be about to improve.

Secret: giving something of ourselves to others is one of the most generous and valuable things that we can do.

In my opinion all human relationships, and I include friend-ships here, should be based on what we offer one another. Some relationships are short and we go our separate ways after we have served that brief purpose to one another. In others that unspoken contract is unfulfilled by both or one of us and these are the sad encounters that can often leave a bitter taste for years after.

Healthy relationships are not possible without gratitude and forgiveness. You cannot have a loving and rewarding relationship with anyone else, much less yourself, if you continue to hold on to things that happened in the past. Regardless of the situation, making peace with past love partners, your parents, children, your brothers and sister, your boss or anyone who you think may have 'done you wrong' is the only way to improve your chances of a 'healthy' relationship with yourself, or anyone else for that matter!

Ghost Stories and Gratitude

In 2005 I was in the south of England, halfway through a lengthy but rewarding tour. There had been some interesting communications along the way. I say 'interesting' because I'd been getting some strong visual images but perhaps none amused or intrigued me more than when I saw a shadowy figure. It may sound almost comical that a psychic medium has this vision but I did and so I was smiling when I asked the audience if they had any idea who this might be.

I explained, 'I've got a gentleman here with me and I don't know if he's talking about himself or someone in the family; would someone please understand about a youngster who used to write ghost stories?'

Almost immediately a man in his thirties put his hand up. 'Yes. When I was a child I used to have a fairly prolific imagination, let's say, and ghost stories were one avenue I used to explore to channel that enthusiasm. With my father's help and encouragement I used to sit down and write.'

'And your name is, sir?'

'Martin.'

'I believe my communication is with your father and that he would help you with those stories.'

'Yes, that's right. Yes.' He nodded.

Martin was next to a woman with the most beautiful head of grey hair I'd seen. I took her to be his mother.

'And you, my love, you're the wife of the man who has passed on.'

'Yes, I am.'

'This is your husband who's communicating to you,' I said. 'He tells me that he knows that one of Martin's earliest memories is of being on a boat.'

'Yes,' said Martin, 'I was sick on a ferry, on a crossing between here and France.'

'Right, I feel as though I need to come over to Mum with this next bit.' I turned to face the lady. 'He's saying that you were right, it was OK to let go. Do you understand? He thinks you were incredibly brave to tell him it was all right to go. Very, very brave.' I listened again as her husband came through with a strong message for her: 'All right sir, I understand – the reason why he has to tell this to you is because he's concerned that you feel you shouldn't have told him to go. But he's saying, "I understand the final words." They were, "Go, John, don't suffer anymore."'

The woman was nodding as I said this. Her voice was tight with emotion as she said, 'It seems that he had a struggle to die. I was near him all the time and I was telling him, "Go, John, go now; don't suffer any more; just go"'; they were the words I actually said to him.'

'I'm now getting a sense of a brother.' I faced Martin and said, 'You have a brother – Robert.'

'Yes.'

'With us, on this side?'

'Yes he is.'

The next question was a difficult one: 'Is your relationship OK?'

'It's not as...' He was unwilling to go on.

'Don't say any more. I've just got to tell you what your dad's saying; he's telling you that he loves you both equally, but you were right to stand up to Robert; you were right to stand your ground because your dad wants you to know that he would have said virtually the same thing. The overpowering sense that I have from your dad is his absolute gratitude that you have looked after your mum.'

Martin smiled. 'He was a great guy, always had my best interests at heart and I miss him very much.'

'I understand the final words. He says you were right to stand up to him,' I concluded.

Martin looked relieved. 'My brother and I had a discussion about Mum's retirement where a few home truths had to be aired and so I'm glad Dad's come through and confirmed what I had to say was right.'

It can be good to know that when we are forced to make tough decisions and stand our ground, we have the backing of our loved ones here and in the afterlife.

 Secret: we need to be able to tell the ones we love the truth otherwise we are not showing our love.

The Starfish

This is one of my favourite stories. It's so simple but it expresses the thought that it does not take much to make a real difference to somebody:

Once upon a time there was a wise man who used to go to the ocean to do his writing. He would walk on the beach early in the morning before he began his work.

One day he was walking along the shore. As he looked down the beach, he saw a human figure moving like a dancer. He smiled to himself to think of someone who would dance to greet the day. So he began to walk faster to catch up.

As he got closer, he saw that the figure was a young man and the young man wasn't dancing; instead he was reaching down to the shore, picking up something and very gently throwing it into the ocean.

As the wise man got closer he called out, 'Good morning! What are you doing?' The young man paused, looked up and replied, 'Throwing starfish in the ocean.'

'I guess I should have asked why are you throwing starfish in the ocean?'

'The sun is up and the tide is going out. And if I don't throw them in they'll die.'

'But, young man, don't you realise that there are miles and miles of beach and starfish all along it. You can't possibly make a difference!'

The young man listened politely. Then bent down, picked another starfish and threw it into the sea, past the breaking waves, and said quietly, 'It made a difference for that one.'

Life can be a challenge; death may be a gift. Socrates said, 'To fear death, gentlemen, is nothing other than to think oneself wise when one is not; for it is to think one knows what one does not know. No man knows whether death may not even turn out to be the greatest of blessings for a human being; yet people fear it as if they knew for certain that it is the greatest of evils.' Perhaps he is right?

Someone who has passed on is in an unfamiliar place. Once they have acclimatised they can see our thoughts of grief, sadness and pain. Remember they are still alive but in a different form. So it's natural that they want to reassure us they are still aware of everything taking place in our physical lives.

The Man Who Retreated into Himself

The occasion was a charity event in the depths of winter. It was a wet and windy night and the short dash from the car into the hall had been enough to get me nearly soaked. So maybe I had this subconscious yearning to be warm and cosy but, as I stood there amongst the milling crowd, I had this picture of some sort of home fire. Quite clearly it seemed to be an oil-burning stove. The image was so strong I felt I had to communicate it, not something I would ever usually do in those circumstances. I found myself turning to a woman who was standing close by. 'Excuse me,' I said and I introduced myself briefly. I explained, 'I'm getting a strong picture here of an oil burning heater of some sort, and it seems to me that someone here has a relative who perhaps fixes them or works with them?'

The woman looked at me in amazement. 'I'm Sandy. It was my father-in-law. He worked for an oil company and serviced the boilers.'

· What I had to say was delicate, but I continued: 'Would you understand when I say that your husband has been very depressed?'

'I would.'

'His dad is aware of your husband's thoughts. He's saying to me that your husband can't see the point.'

Sandy sighed audibly before replying, 'Yes, he's having trouble seeing the wood for the trees. There are a few pressures that he's had through work and there are a few medical problems going round the family at the moment, so yes, that's all very accurate. When my father-in-law died it was a very difficult time for everybody, and for some time before his death he knew what was going to happen. My husband would say he was the bravest man, even though he knew what the consequences were.'

'Tell your husband this from his dad: "I never gave in so you're not going to give in."'

'Right. Well, that makes sense.' Sandy seemed to be hearing what she already knew, but that is often the way when we hear communications from the afterlife.

A young woman I took to be Sandy's daughter was standing next to her. She looked at me with wide-eyed astonishment as I turned to her and said, 'You're the granddaughter of the gentleman who has passed over.'

'Yes, I'm Michelle.'

'Are you and your dad quite close?'

'Yes, now we are, yes.'

'Your grandfather was a lovely man, wasn't he darling?'

Michelle smiled. She clearly had lots of happy thoughts; you could see it in her eyes as she spoke: 'He was an absolutely wonderful man. He passed over when I was fourteen so I don't remember too much about him, but I do remember the infectious laugh that he had; he filled the room with laughter. Just a wonderful, happy, big man that you felt safe with all the time.'

At that point Sandy chipped in: 'He was the sort of person who, if you arrived or left the house and you didn't give him a kiss goodbye, he'd want to know why.'

'Michelle my love, will you take your dad out, sit him down and tell him his dad has said he's got to stop thinking about your grandpa so negatively, but most importantly he must stop thinking only about himself? He needs to look outwards.'

'I certainly will,' she agreed. At that point an announcement drew our attention and we joined the rest of the crowd.

For those unfamiliar with the world of mediums I don't want to give the impression that it's all doom and gloom when we communicate. Often there are people in the audience who come with no particular need or issue, and when they receive a communication from their loved ones they can be quite relaxed. For me, these people appear quite spiritual: that is, they have learned to believe in the bigger picture and accept what has happened. Their contact with death has awakened them to the fact that some day they too will pass into the spirit. Because of that they are in a position to think about other things. For example, how might they live their lives in harmony or in a more meaningful way? How might they improve their spiritual life? Of course they don't refer to their life in that way but I can always tell that these people have a positive way about them. And that is a very pleasing part of my work.

Secret: even though we may want to focus on those who have passed over, we must also remember we have a duty to this life and the people who are still in it. Our loved ones communicate from the other side to strengthen not only their relationships with us, but to motivate the strengthening of earthly relationships.

A Colourful Life

It had been a busy evening, with lots of communications. However, there was still a lot of energy bouncing round the room, and it felt like a good place to be.

I walked over to speak to the people on the right-hand side of the audience: 'I'm sort of being pulled down here; I'm in these two front rows. Would someone here please understand about a father or grandfather figure here who used to tell a story about a person who used to have their hand nailed to a table? And I'm getting this reference to a pub, The Three Barrels or three…'

'That'll be The Three Crowns,' said a gruff voice.

'Would you know what I'm talking about?' I moved closer towards the speaker.

'Yes, I'm pretty sure,' the man's voice said confidently.

'OK, just step forward a little, sir…'

'Alan's the name.'

'All right, Alan, and there was an unlucky guy who had his hand impaled or nailed to a table.'

'That was a connection to my dad's best friend.'

'And your dad has passed to the spirit, sir.'

'Yes, he has,' Alan confirmed.

'There's actually something, sir – blimey, it's a good job it's a long time ago! I think this is a bit naughty actually: somebody used to doctor barrels of beer.'

Alan didn't reply so I continued, 'OK, I don't want to talk about watered-down beer, but I do want to talk about this particular place, because he seems to have very vivid and fond memories of it. It was like a second home. A very lively place indeed.'

Alan chuckled. 'That'd be about right!'

'So what's this about your dad nailing a hand to a table?'

'The Three Crowns pub is one of the public houses that

my dad and his mates used to drink in as young lads and one of the first places he took my mum for a drink when they started courting. He and his mate were always up to pranks – nothing nasty but they did get themselves into a bit of danger. They were doing that thing where you stab the knife into the table between someone's fingers. Anyway, Dad put his hand on the table and they did it and it was OK. But when Dad tried to do it to his mate, he missed and stabbed him, quite badly, in the back of the hand.'

Quite a party trick! I moved on: 'All right, he's letting me know that there was something important to him, that he had an attachment or item carved out of a material like dark stone. It's a bit of carving of some sort.'

Alan understood straightaway what I was talking about. 'Well, you see,' he said, 'Dad was an ex-miner, and he carved this thing out of an old piece of coal. It was actually from a piece of old rock out of the pit, and it was very, very hard, from the rock face. He carved a little miner out of it. Mum has still got the miner to this day, which is a treasured memory, a family heirloom, so to speak.'

'What was this situation where your dad ended up to here in water?' I raised my hand to my chest level, adding, 'And his life was in danger.'

'He was trapped for seventy-two hours in a pit,' Alan replied.

'In water? For seventy-two hours?' It sounded terrible, and there were sounds of 'oh dear!' and 'ooh' from the audience as you'd expect.

'Yes, it was a dreadful situation,' Alan agreed.

'And the water began to rise and by the time they got him out, he had his head above water still,' I said, the images filling my mind.

'Just. It was just above the water.'

'Just above the water. All right, and who got foot rot?' I asked, adding, 'He's telling me about that but I can't tell who it is. There was an accident involved.'

'It was an accident I had on a motorbike and my foot turned,' Alan explained. 'It happened when I was seventeen and I'd done a few dares on my bike along with my mates. It all ended badly when I came to a sudden stop against a very solid brick wall. I was in a coma and had my spleen removed, and needless to say I was in a very bad way for a good while. It was pretty bad.' There were more 'eeks' and 'oohs' from the audience.

Alan went on: 'My ankle became infected and when my dad saw it, he said, "You've got foot rot, lad!"'

'Your dad was a jokey character, I must say,' I smiled. 'He says you were never quite big enough for a Norton or a Triumph. He seems to be taunting you. He's saying, "Son, your legs were never quite long enough."'

'Well, that'd definitely be my dad. He was only five feet three!'

'Now he's actually talking about the garden. He's saying that you've got to dig up the dahlias and not put them in until next year.'

'The gardening came from my grandad,' said Alan, 'because he was a fanatical gardener, and no matter what the flower or plant, he could give you the Latin name for it and tell you all about it. He was just so red hot on it.'

I continued: 'You've either got a pond you want to make bigger or you want to put a pond in the garden... It concerns someone else and your dad is saying you should get on with it!'

Alan chuckled again. 'Susan, my wife, has been going on and on about digging this pond, and I always find an excuse to try and get out of doing it, but it looks like she's going to get her own way now, because Dad says I have to do it. So, thanks, Dad!'

Alan told me later that the aspect of his father he'd remembered most was that he was a true family man, whose main concern was to look after his family. He'd always told them that was why he was there and it made him proud to be able to do it. It was clear to me that his dad had been strict on his children and never took any nonsense but was also a very loving, classic old-school parent.

Alan commented, 'My father passed away last October 13th and it was this huge, massive shock to the family and everyone else. Within a six week period he went from being fit and quite healthy – though he obviously had his problems – to someone we couldn't recognise. Within those six weeks he had deteriorated to such a condition that he wasn't my dad, and within two to three days he had passed on. But,' added Alan, 'he was always there for us.'

Secret: if we are able to accept the reality of physical death we will feel closer to those who have passed over and they in turn will feel less inhibited about connecting with us.

When I'm standing in front of a studio or theatre audience waiting to begin I invariably start thinking about the types of communications that might come through. While I'm often the bearer of happy words and specific instructions that make me and others feel good, I think sometimes it's what I call the 'release' messages that are the most rewarding. These sorts of messages often involve people who have shared so much with someone else that it's extremely hard for them to continue when that person passes over. They cannot do the things they previously did because those activities are inextricably linked to their loved ones, and so they feel lost. These are situations where those who are left behind are carrying a huge burden, not really of their own making, and they can find no way out. They need to be set free and sometimes a simple but important communication from the afterlife can achieve that.

The Adventurer's Widow

As I stood waiting for the show to start, I watched the audience enter. I like to watch people, to see their anticipation and the expressions on their faces. It gives me some sort of idea of the mood of the crowd. From what I could see we had a very smartly dressed gathering that day!

My first contact was a very strong personality who had some very specific memories he wanted to share with the much-loved wife he'd left behind; a wife who was finding the new emptiness in her life very difficult to deal with, like many people who've lost loved ones do.

I found myself focusing on an elegant but frail-looking woman. She was impeccably attired in navy and white. I guessed she was in her sixties but she had a well-to-do look about her and a light tan that suggested she spent a lot of time outdoors. I invited her to join me and take a seat on the sofa under the studio lights.

'May I ask your name?' I asked.

'It's Maggie,' she replied in a no-nonsense manner.

'Maggie, there's someone here who sails a boat. I'm seeing a man in a yachtsman's hat. Tell me, your husband isn't still with us on this side of life, is he?'

'No, he's not.' She half shook her head as if to say she'd no idea where he was.

'So he's passed over. Did you both sail?

'Yes.'

'Did your husband go on a helicopter trip or a helicopter ride?'

'Well yes, my husband did so.'

'I get the feeling, Maggie,' I said, 'that I should mention his secret desire to have a pilot's licence.'

'I wouldn't be surprised at that at all!' She smiled fondly at the thought.

'He's giving me the sense of a man that would like to do things that you would normally associate with a younger person; there's an irrepressible, adventurous spirit in him,' I explained.

'Well, we've been involved in sailing for twenty years, dinghies for ten, cruisers for another ten. My husband was very young at heart. When I first met him he was a racing cyclist, racing for England – he'd had to put his career on hold while we got married – but while we were married he involved himself in helicopter rides, skiing, sailing, windsurfing – you name it, he did it.'

I paused. 'Maggie, I'm wondering about something here. In the latter part of his life, was it you or him that was suffering from headaches?'

Maggie raised a neat eyebrow. 'The headaches belonged to me.'

'Ah, it's you. So you understand why he's putting a cup or glass of hot water in my mind?'

'Yes, I do,' Maggie affirmed. 'The very last words we exchanged before Tony died were when I asked him to get me a glass of hot water, and he said, "I didn't bring you one because you'd already gone to bed."'

'Maggie, I have the feeling he didn't expect to go when he did.' At that moment this stylish, dignified woman looked a little forlorn but she was clearly doing her best to keep it all together. I continued with the communication he was giving me: 'I know there was something that went wrong in the chest, and the most obvious thing for me to say is the heart. Because the thought that he's giving me now was he didn't know he was having a heart attack. It wasn't – I think this is where the shock or surprise came in – because it didn't feel like what a heart attack would feel like.'

Maggie nodded, having recovered her composure. 'Yes, that's absolutely right. We'd gone to bed as normal; my husband had earlier spoken to 120 people at a function at lunch time, and when we went to bed I was woken up at 4 o'clock, just in time to hear the last signs of my husband, if you like, and then he died. When I spoke to the police afterwards, I couldn't believe how beautiful the whole affair had been, tragic but calm and so beautiful.'

I smiled. 'I think this is almost a bit cheeky really, or a bit tongue-in-cheek; he's so pleased you haven't moved too much in the house or on the boat. He's quite touched by the fact that everything is more or less as it was.'

'It is – I haven't touched anything,' Maggie admitted.

'Well, your husband is obviously very charming and cheeky then: he's saying some habits do change because he'd often say to you, "What have you done with…"'

Maggie laughed and there was a sparkle in her eyes.

'Very, very nice sense of humour,' I continued. 'He's saying, "I've had to pass over to get you to stop moving stuff!"'

'I've left everything alone, and the reason why I've done that is because it's like somebody has gone out shopping and not come back. Until I know within myself that I'm ready to move things about, then I will.'

'Tell me, Maggie,' I said, 'he seems to be showing me an area that looks like marshes, and I just feel that this is like a favourite area for him, or a place that you both loved very much; lots of references to water, because I see lots of water-type birds, wading-type birds.'

Maggie nodded again. 'We used to go to a place in Sussex where there are all those birds and nature reserves. It's one of our favourite spots, and the sky is absolutely wonderful. I think I will have to be ready, emotionally, when I go there, and I do hope it will help me to feel closer to my husband.'

'He says he would be right there with you if you walked that area again. It's just something that stays with him as a place that you both loved very much. He is telling me that he came today for no other reason than to express his wishes to you; express his love to you, and the words that he's leaving with you are: "There are a lot worse ways to die." I believe, from what he's tried to show me, that he didn't want a long, lingering death, so in that respect, he feels he got his wish. A very, very nice man.'

Maggie made a little gesture of acknowledgment, and for a second I caught a glimmer of the girl her husband had fallen in love with all those years ago.

Secret: the abrupt manner of a loved one's passing does not affect in any way the relationship we had or continue to have with them.

Give and take – that is an essential part of loving friendships and relationships. Giving to friends and loved ones also means being able to say what you really think and if you are truly friends, the other person should be able to take what you tell them in the right way – provided you say it constructively of course. Friendships and relationships are not just about taking the good, the 'fun bits' as it were. They're about honesty and respect and having enough of both to tell someone what you really think.

A Lively Lady

'I've got a connection here; I've got this gentleman talking about doing "the knowledge". The only sense I can make of this is that it's what you do when you're learning to become a taxi driver and memorising all the streets in London. But this gentleman used to get hopelessly lost!'

A woman in the front row of the theatre started giggling and nodding her head vigorously.

I focused on her and smiled. 'I'm guessing, love, that's it you we're talking about. Just a wild guess, you understand!'

'Yes, that would be me. My name is Carol.'

'Now Carol, darling, do you remember a phone call taking place, saying, "I'm somewhere but I don't know where I am"?'

Once again Carol started giggling and this time others joined in with her. You could see she was a woman who enjoyed a good time. It's fun to have people like her in the *6ixth Sense* studio audience as they help to bring everyone together and create a relaxed atmosphere. As long as they don't laugh too much, which puts people off!

I continued, 'I've got to say, and it's probably an inappropriate thing to say, but I've got this fellow linking with me who is killing himself laughing. A bit like you actually.'

Carol suddenly stopped giggling and looked ahead, concentrating hard.

'My love, there's a memory here of gasping for air, as if he is trying to show me that at the end he had this need to gasp for air,' I explained. 'And this is very strange, but this man half feels like family and half doesn't. Can you understand why he feels close to you, but it doesn't quite feel quite right to say family? It was almost like families that were very friendly with each other.'

Carol nodded. 'Yes, well sort of friendly…let's call it an uneasy peace,' she said.

'Right. Now I'm getting a sense of three fellows. Who were three fellows that used to go off to amateur boxing matches?'

'Oh, that would be Matthew, Johnny and Rocky Harley,' Carol confirmed. 'It could only be them.'

As we talked – Carol, the man's spirit and I – it turned out that the Harley boys belonged to a very well-known family who were known for causing trouble in the neighbourhood. The head of the family, a fellow called Terry Harley, was a classic patriarch – a bit like a mafia godfather, according to Carol, and it was him I had the connection with now. She said that the reference to his being half family was because there had been an incident when her son and one of his grandsons got into trouble in a very serious way which had linked both of their families. As Carol herself put it, 'We got a nice connection out of something bad, and something good came out of it.'

'And you know about the fight breaking out in a pub with glasses flying everywhere, don't you?' I said. The audience let out a little collective gasp.

'Oh yes, Colin!' Carol covered her mouth with her hand in surprise.

'Right, OK. There was some old dear who they put under the pub table because there were glasses flying everywhere. But she kept popping up and throwing a bottle and they had to keep pulling her back down underneath the table because there was all hell breaking loose in this pub, with glasses flying everywhere. She kept popping up and I can see this stack of Babycham bottles, and these Babycham bottles went flying!'

'You're letting my secrets out now!' Carol exclaimed.

'Back to the coffin and the funeral now,' I said, moving swiftly on. 'The coffin was actually drawn through the streets on the back of a brewer's dray.'

'That's right,' said Carol. 'It's the only funeral that I've ever seen with the coffin on the back of a cart. Well, it was more elegant than a cart, I suppose, but the horse was a large old boy. And Terry was a big man himself, both in a physical sense and because of his personality. The funeral was Romany, gypsy. It was a bit austere – would that be the word? But it was very fitting for him.'

'Well, he's saying he respected you because you were the only one brave enough to tell him what you thought,' I explained.

'Yes, I can be a bit gutsy really,' Carol giggled. 'Sometimes too much for my own good.'

'And he might well have told you that you were an interfering so and so ... but you were the only one that would tell him what you really thought!'

'Yes, you see I wasn't afraid of him. I'm not afraid of anyone ... not even you, Colin.' There was an audible titter from the audience.

'You're a cheeky old so-and-so!' I laughed. 'Also, he says, "There are some people that would be pleased, or not pleased, to know that I'm not actually burning in the fires of hell!" I think if you passed that message on where it's supposed to go they'll understand why it's been given to them!'

'Oh, that's meant for me! One in the eye from him!' Carol exclaimed, almost indignantly.

'Yes, because you said "You'll burn! You'll burn!" and he's saying, "Well, I'm not actually burning in the fires of hell and I'm doing all right!" But he did actually like you and he had a lot of time for you. He says you have a lot of spirit.'

Carol said that this all went back to that time when her eldest son had got into a fracas with one of Terry's grandsons. The boys in the family had a policy that if one of them was knocked down then the next eldest would get involved. Unfortunately, her next son had become caught up in the fight too and was hurt quite badly, with broken ribs. Carol had been so angry she had gone round to the Harley household and started kicking the door – which was apparently something nobody in the neighbourhood dared to even *think* of doing.

'When they came to the door I confronted them! I just felt I needed to stand my ground,' Carol explained. 'The fact that he's come through to me today has gobsmacked me, that's all I can say. But now I'll go round to see his wife Ginger and tell her.'

Carol left that day knowing that somebody in the afterlife would always respect her feisty spirit and courage.

Secret: honesty and respect transcend earthly conflicts.

For me, giving is an essential part of my being and I don't mean giving material things or what I do for a living. I mean the sort of give and take that is the part of loving friendships and relationships. Giving to friends and loved ones also means being able to say what you really think. If you are truly friends, the other person should be able to take what you tell them in the right way – provided you say it constructively of course.

I certainly didn't envisage that in my forties I would find myself with the best friends I have had in my life, some of whom I have known for years. Our friendships have endured the passage of time and I believe this is largely because we have never asked more from one another than we are able to give. These relationships – and I use the word broadly, not just about sexual relationships – are based on mutual respect and understanding. New friends have brought with them new adventure and have encouraged me to value different types of people and to be bolder in my life, rather than just stick to the tried and tested.

All of our relationships need to grow with us; we cannot expect them to stay fixed forever, and this also applies to those we have loved who have passed. For our relationships and friendships to change, we may have to be brave and draw upon inner strength. Love can help us to do this, and so can another important secret that the afterlife teaches us: hope.

2 | Secrets of Hope

I BELIEVE that, in the large majority of cases, for many of us who are not getting from life what we truly want and desire, we ourselves are part of the problem. I have found, both in my personal life and from observing other people, that we get what we wish for, whether we consciously wish for it or not. We are all to a great extent in charge of our reality and that means we're responsible for our hopes and dreams and for putting them into action.

I have a friend who sometimes complains, 'I never meet the right man.' So I say to her, 'Well, where did you meet the last one? You went to a club; you knew nothing about each other. You went to bed together and then you saw each for three months. You broke up probably because you met one another under the wrong circumstances. Then you return to the nightclub to repeat the behaviour.' She knew what I was saying. The fact is that we are often as responsible for the negative experiences in our lives as we are for the good things that come our way.

While my life is certainly not idyllic (when it comes down to it nobody's life is perfect), I am lucky enough to do something I enjoy almost every day and I'm grateful for that. I'm writing this having recently returned from Madrid where I saw someone I hadn't seen for twenty-two years. He is a fair bit older than me but we've been great friends for a long time. We were talking about the good old days, the bad old days and everything in between. I told him I wouldn't change a single thing in my life and he agreed it was the same for him. Our bad experiences have been opportunities for us to grow in some way and so they were necessary. At some point in your life, hopefully at a young enough age, you reach an understanding that adverse experiences can eventually lead to something good. The old saying of 'one door closes, another one opens' is something I've found to be utterly, indisputably true.

Something else that is true is that most of the time people expect life to happen to them instead of taking charge of it themselves. The way I see it, they are following life around instead of leading it. Instead of taking responsibility they point to others and say, 'Look it's his/her fault. They are to blame for my dreams not coming true.' I think that's all part of the victim mentality that is so prevalent in society today. It's easy to believe there is always someone else whose responsibility it is to make life better for us or to take charge of our happiness and desires. I've believed it too at times; we all have. But once you go through a period of self-awareness and come out the other end you realise that it's up to you. And, guess what? It's not so bad. It's actually exciting knowing you're in charge of your own life. You are free to choose. And it's all out there. I find that such a wonderful, amazing thought – all those possibilities.

As for what we hope for, well that's easy. In a nutshell, we all want happiness. But if we want it so badly why can't we find it? Ah, but we can. As part of our ability to choose we can choose to feel happy. By the way that doesn't mean laughing and jumping up and down all the time. What is happiness? It's a feeling of inner peace and satisfaction. It's usually experienced when there are no worries, fears or obsessing thoughts, and this usually happens when we do something we love to do or when we obtain, win or achieve something that we value. It seems to be the outcome of positive events, but it actually comes from the inside, triggered by our response to external events.

My own observations tell me that most of us feel especially happy when we have offered something of ourselves to others, when we've been able to ease another person's suffering, and when we are content with what we already have in our lives. We feel best when we experience love, optimism, courage, a sense of freedom and purpose. But the blatant, obvious truth is that we don't always get what we hope for when we want it. Despite what the world of self-help tells us, merely wanting something badly enough does not mean we stand a chance of getting it. Does this mean that we must lose all hope? No, because one thing I have learned from my work is that we carry hope inside us. It's an essential part of the human spirit that can offer a great deal of comfort in difficult times.

A Message of Comfort

I stood before a small group – I guess about fifty people – at a demonstration that had been organised by a spiritualist group I had long-standing connections to. There was an air of anticipation in the room and, with far fewer people than in my studio or theatre readings, a very cosy feeling of intimacy as well. I looked into the group – you wouldn't call it a crowd – and picked out a woman whom I felt I was being strongly drawn to.

'My love, you've got a brother on the spirit side of life.' I said to her.

The woman, whose name was Lisa, acknowledged that she did.

'I also sense your mum is on this side of life,' I noted.

'Yes,' said Lisa with a tone of surprise in her voice. Surprise and amazement are reactions you often get when you ask people about loved ones who are still in this earthly world. Everyone assumes that medium communications talk exclusively about those who've passed over, but we don't.

'I feel that this is for you and your mum, my darling. Who nearly passed out at the funeral? It was an older lady, wasn't it?'

'It was my mother,' Lisa replied.

'Your brother – I'm getting the name Paul or Pete – seems to be strongly aware that your mother had a very difficult time at the funeral. Are you with the lady next to you?

'Yes.'

I turned to her. 'And tell me, madam, you're connected to Mum, aren't you?

The lady sitting to Lisa's left replied, 'Yes, I'm Sandra and I'm connected to Lisa through being her sister-in-law.'

'So you're connected to Mum as well. Was there pain in her abdomen, Lisa?'

'Oh, yes, quite a lot actually.' Lisa frowned sadly, as though she was recalling difficult memories.

'All right, because he's giving me the feeling there was pain here, but there obviously isn't any pain now.' I touched my chest before looking at the two women again. 'Who's having the tests for suspected angina?' I wondered.

'My mother.'

'All right, he says, "She's been playing up like a good 'un recently." Look, you've got to tell your mum this from your brother; she's got to do as she's told because he's not ready for her yet. OK? She's got to stop this thing of saying, "Well, if I went, nobody would miss me anyway." He's saying tell her to stop being so stupid; of course people would miss her.' I turned to Sandra. 'Tell me, my love, is your husband his brother?'

'Yes,' she said.

'Hmm, he's done something to his joints. Knees ... perhaps back.'

'Yes, it's his back. He put it out.'

'The pain must be travelling from the back down the leg, and it's coming down the foot.'

'That's right, yes,' Sandra agreed.

'My love, is your husband frightened of needles? Not injections, needles like acupuncture needles.'

Sandra grinned. 'Yes, he's pathetic! He's absolutely terrified.' The audience gave a soft murmur and there were a few giggles.

'So is this acupuncture he's talking about to me?'

'No, he wouldn't have that.'

'But someone has suggested it, haven't they? Right, OK, because what your brother-in-law's actually showing me is that if your husband wasn't so frightened of needles he could have acupuncture all right. And he might feel better. Your brother just wants you to know that he keeps an eye on the family. Unfortunately, I feel that your mum will not listen to anybody like she'd listen to him.'

Lisa agreed with this and Sandra added, 'My husband is frightened of needles, but the fact that Pete has said that it would be beneficial for him means that he might just go and do it now.'

'I feel that's why he's drawn forward today, so you can go home and say, "Now look, Mum, he's said you've got to start doing as you're told," because if he was here she would listen to him. He's saying, "Well, I might not be here in body, but I'm still here all right, and I want her to start doing as she's told and stop this nonsense; stop saying that if she went no one would miss her."'

Lisa recounted the story of how her brother had passed. 'My brother Pete went to work as usual. He was putting some tiles on a roof and apparently he was up there when he had a massive heart attack; he was very young, just thirty-five years old. He's left three little children, which is very hard for them and us. We were so very close; you know, he lived just round the corner from us and we saw each other daily so it's really left a huge gap in our lives. My mum's had angina for a few years, but since Pete's passing she's been having more and more attacks.'

'Well, ladies,' I explained, 'he's very, very adamant: she's got to stop this victim mentality where she thinks that she doesn't matter and that if she was not around she wouldn't be missed. He's had enough of hearing that.'

'Everybody does love her, and we're all behind her,' said Lisa. 'It's just very early days at the moment, and it's not something a mother expects – I mean to lose a child who is a fit, healthy man to a disease that you expect someone much older to get. Plus he was the youngest, her baby. But we will tell her about him coming through and I have a feeling she might listen.'

'He just wants you to know that he keeps an eye on the family.'

Lisa nodded and smiled. 'It's very comforting to know that he is there, watching over us, and especially watching over his mum because that would be a great comfort to her.'

Secret: loved ones who have passed over are still there to guide and instruct us. We just have to listen and look for the signs.

It's our attitude that makes us feel happy or unhappy. If you think about an average day, in the space of those twenty-four hours you'll encounter all kinds of situations, some of which may not be ideal in terms of contributing to your happiness. However, you can choose to keep thinking about the annoying or irritating events or not. All of us constantly go through various situations and circumstances, but we do not have to let them influence our reactions and feelings. Let me tell you, I don't always find this easy and it's by no means automatic with me. However, I do try to make the effort to stop and think, 'How do I want this parking ticket or broken window or stupid disagreement to influence my life? Hang on, let me block out the noise and hubbub for a moment.' If I manage to do that I generally end up taking a more relaxed approach and feeling more peaceful as a result.

If we let external events influence our moods, we become their slaves and lose our freedom. Instead of allowing our happiness to be determined by these external forces, we can decide to turn our backs on them. What I personally think it boils down to is rather simple really: we need to tap into our free spirit, the part of us that sees joy and light in life.

As you've read earlier in this book, one of the special features we did occasionally on the *6ixth Sense* show was to invite people who've already had readings in the past to return and see what has happened since. This might sound like every reading I do is life-changing, which isn't so. Many of the messages that I pass on seem very simple messages but they are nevertheless important to the person who receives them. However, even the messages that are more substantial don't necessarily require that the person or people who receive the communication go off and turn their lives upside down. What I do hope for many of these people is that they somehow realise that:

- Our thoughts are very powerful things
- Our thoughts and emotions affect everything around us and have a wider influence than we imagine
- Each of us has access to a power that is unlimited, and there for the asking. It can provide us with answers, assistance and guidance. The power is within us all.
- We are creators of our own futures for the benefit of ourselves, our friends, family and society as a whole.

Harry Finds his Softer Side

Harry and Beverly live in Leyton and were in the audience for a previous series where Harry was both shocked and surprised to receive an emotionally charged message from his father who had passed some years before. The message itself centred around Harry's dad saying that although he felt he hadn't been all bad, he thought he could have been a much better father to his family.

As Harry put it, 'When we went to see the show I was very sceptical. To be quite honest, I really thought this was a load of codswallop and didn't believe in what you did at all. I mean, honestly, this stuff about mediums sounded so far fetched to me, but Beverly persuaded me that it was worth coming along so I thought, "What's the harm in it?" And then when it started to unfold you made some amazing revelations and, yeah, you frightened the life out of me too!'

Also in the audience that day was their grown-up daughter, Hayley, who felt the reading had a positive impact on her father's relationship with the family. As she told the assembled audience: 'He has definitely changed for the better in many ways, one of them being that he will now discuss his feelings with us and won't shy away from them like he did before.'

I told them that it took very strong a brave man to admit when he was wrong.

'Believe me, Colin, I've done that a lot in the past year – in fact more than I've probably done in my whole life,' said Harry.

I asked him if that same behaviour applied to his relationship with his daughter.

Hayley chipped in: 'After hearing from his father, my dad admitted he was wrong in the way he'd acted towards me and my husband Alan. We'd separated after a few very difficult years and neither of us had found it plain sailing. We still loved each other very much and decided we'd like to give our relationship another try, which wasn't easy as there was all this stuff we had to get through. And I guess what I wanted was some sort of encouragement from Dad even if I didn't exactly have his blessing. Dad was really resentful when me and Alan split up, which is fair enough, but I expected him to want what I wanted. Anyway, after we came to the *6ixth Sense* and he got that message from his father, he changed his attitude completely. It was lovely because up till then you could never have got my dad to say sorry.'

'Well,' I said, 'life could have been much easier for you too, Harry, if your father had admitted you were right and he was wrong when he was.'

'Yes,' said Harry, 'and now I'm seeing that it's all right to admit that you're wrong. It doesn't mean you lose control or are any less manly or whatever. And there's no way in hell I would've done it before the reading.'

I suggested to him that because his own father had showed him how proud he was, this had helped him to reach into himself and make the effort he needed to create and develop a better relationship with his daughter. 'Your father said at the time he just couldn't say the words "I love you" in his earthly life, and I think that really affected you,' I observed.

'I can't tell you how much that threw me,' said Harry. 'One minute I was wondering why I was here listening to what I thought was rubbish and the next I heard that. It really was something. The question of whether Dad loved us or not when we were kids really tormented me because I never knew.'

'You made my dad very happy,' Hayley said to me. 'It also made him quite sad because I think he wished he'd known earlier. Since the reading he's been more open. He even cuddles my brother!'

'Is that so, Harry?' I wondered, feeling very pleased for him.

Harry gave a little gulp and then said proudly, 'Yes, he's a grown-up man and six foot four inches tall, but now I'm prepared to tell him I love him and give him a hug.'

I also asked Harry how he felt about being told in that earlier reading that he had not passed over due to heart attack because his dad felt he needed to stay in the physical world and continue.

Harry looked very thoughtful. 'I've actually had another heart attack since then, but, you know Colin, I'm not afraid now because this has taught me there's something more after we pass over.'

Ripples

I enjoy stories and parables that have come to us through the ages. In a relatively short space of words – and in a very clever way – they convey deep secrets. This is one such story that has some wise things to say about responsibility to our loved ones.

The Master was walking through the fields one day when a young man, with a troubled look upon his face, approached him.

'On such a beautiful day, it must be difficult to stay so serious,' the Master said.

'Is it? I hadn't noticed,' the young man said, turning to look around and notice his surroundings. His eyes scanned the landscape, but nothing seemed to register; his mind was elsewhere. Watching intently, the Master continued to walk.

'Join me if you like,' he offered. He walked to the edge of a still pond framed by sycamore trees, their leaves golden orange and about to fall.

'Please sit down,' the Master invited, patting the ground next to him. Looking carefully before sitting, the young man brushed the ground to clear a space for himself.

'Now, find a small stone, please,' the Master instructed.

'What?'

'A stone. Please find a small stone and throw it in the pond.'

Searching around him, the young man grabbed a pebble and threw it as far as he could.

'Tell me what you see,' the Master instructed.

Straining his eyes to not miss a single detail, the man looked at the water's surface. 'I see ripples.'

'Where did the ripples come from?'

'From the pebble I threw in the pond, Master.'

'Please reach your hand into the water and stop the ripples,' the Master said.

Not understanding, the young man stuck his hand in the water as a ripple neared, only to cause more ripples. The young man was now completely baffled. Where was this going? Had he made a mistake in seeking out the Master? Puzzled, the young man waited.

'Were you able to stop the ripples with your hands?' the Master asked.

'No, of course not.'

'Could you have stopped the ripples, then?'

'No, Master. I told you – I only caused more ripples.'

'What if you had stopped the pebble from entering the water to begin with?' The Master smiled such a beautiful smile, the young man could not be upset.

The Master continued, 'Next time you are unhappy with your life, catch the stone before it hits the water. Do not spend time trying to undo what you have done. Rather, change what you are going to do before you do it.' The Master looked kindly upon the young man.

'But Master, how will I know what I am going to do before I do it?'

'Take the responsibility for living your own life. If you're working with a doctor to treat an illness, then ask the doctor to help you understand what caused the illness. Do not just treat the ripples. Keep asking questions.'

The young man stopped, his mind reeling. 'But I came to you to ask you for answers. Are you saying that I know the answers?'

'You may not know the answers right now, but if you ask the right questions, then you shall discover the answers.'

'But what are the right questions, Master?'

'There are no wrong questions, only unasked ones. We must ask, for without asking, we cannot receive answers. But it is your responsibility to ask. No one else can do that for you.' With that, the Master rose to his feet and slowly walked away through the autumn trees, a secret smile playing on his lips.

Secret: we need not repeat the mistakes of those who have passed; nor should we resent them for those mistakes. If we repeat misguided patterns of behaviour then we are responsible for our actions, not them!

At the time of death, the physical body falls away from the consciousness, or spirit, leaving it with no option but to seek out where to go and what to do next. The immediate reactions of the spirit are determined by its thoughts and ideas of when it lived within the body. This means that your own thoughts and the way you have lived your life will determine how you will spend your time in the afterlife. Why is that? The answer is simply that a negative individual, on this plane or the next, is carried through their life on a much coarser, heavier vibration than a positive one. Perhaps you've heard a friend say that they like to be with so-and-so because that person always lifts their spirits and cheers them up. This is because that person is a warm and positive individual whose presence rubs off on those around them.

Among other things, psychic mediumship, which I practise, can heal. I don't mean it can make you physically well but what it can do is bring some calm and peace of mind to people who feel they have unfinished business. While this can sometimes be a huge life-long argument unresolved, much of the time I find that it's little things that are bothering people. Quite often these things will only surface after a loved one has passed over; it's only then that they become important. And if the one who has passed over feels the time is right, they will come through. I'm very careful not to raise people's expectations of what might happen: even mediums do not know everything! Nor can we sense everything and everyone who has passed over.

An Unexpected Surprise

Some of the members of my audiences are really quite specific about what they're hoping for. As I've often said, I try not to raise people's expectations either in private sittings or during shows. Sarah, I found out later on, had come to watch the show hoping to get in contact with her uncle who had brought her up. However, the reason she came to my attention was that I'd felt the presence of a man who was estranged from his family who wasn't her uncle. But she knew exactly who it was. She put her hand up when she heard the description of the man.

'Hello darling, what's your name?' I asked.

'Sarah.'

'Sarah, has your dad passed over?'

Sarah said she believed he had but she wasn't sure.

'And your mother. Is she with you?' I wondered.

'No, she has passed over.'

'Ah, right,' I said, 'I think we're getting a little bit of a mystery here.'

'Yes...' she began but I stopped her in mid-sentence. When a communication comes through it's important to let it run its course so that nothing else clouds it. Sometimes people try to clarify things early on for me, but I'd honestly prefer that they didn't.

Now it was becoming clearer. 'No, it's OK, an absent father,' I said. 'If it helps you, because I'm sure that it will and because your mother was always affected by it throughout her life, your mother and father have made some peace between themselves on the other side of life.'

'Oh, gosh. Really?' Sarah blinked a couple of times. 'I would never have expected it from the way they were together. They were constantly bickering.' She seemed genuinely surprised.

'I understand. Given the way your mother's putting this through to me, there was always this remnant of bitterness towards your father while she was on this side of life.'

Sarah nodded in agreement. 'Yes, Colin, there was. But she didn't have an easy time to begin with.'

As we talked it became clear that Sarah's mother had been an extraordinary woman. Apparently, she'd had a troubled life as a young woman in Bulgaria. Her life had started out comfortably as her family had been very well off and her mother was regarded as one of the most beautiful women around; she was a young, glamorous girl around town who played tennis. Hers was a good life. Then the Second World War broke out and of course everything changed. Her mother ended up in a work camp where she suffered, and watched many others suffer, in the most dreadful and heartbreaking way. After this she found her way to England, where she met Sarah's father.

'Darling, she wants you to know that having both passed to the other side of life, there is a wonderful and loving peace between them, so much so that they've been able to draw close together today to be able to communicate with you.'

At that moment Sarah put her head in her hands and I was a bit concerned. When she looked up she didn't have tears in her eyes as I expected, but she looked a bit bewildered. 'You look a bit shocked, my darling,' I observed.

'I'm quite surprised since my father left home when I was little and I really didn't have any contact with him at all from about the age of four upwards. The idea that they have once again got in touch – in a positive way – is quite a lot to take in. It was probably something I'd hoped for at the back of my mind, but hadn't dared think of.'

'Now Sarah, take a deep breath, darling. I must tell you she's saying she appreciates what you had to do at the end. She was quite happy there, at that place. She's saying you mustn't have any feelings that she should've have been anywhere else.'

Sarah looked relieved. 'Thank goodness for that. I felt tremendously bad about her going into a hospice but it was really all I could do. I know she said, "It's all right, they're putting on a few shows and everything's all right, and I'm

OK to be here." But I still felt guilty so that's really good to hear.'

'Now tell me, darling; did your mother have very nice hands?'

Sarah looked taken aback at the question. 'Well yes, as it happens...'

'Because I can see the most beautiful, long, elegant hands,' I explained.

Sarah smiled. 'Yes, I'd always look at her hands and think, "They're so beautiful," and they were soft and lovely right until the end, which is quite unusual for an older person since ... well, you know ... the hands are the first to go.'

'Goodness Sarah, I certainly do!' I laughed. 'Well, my love, you can stop wringing your own hands because she knows you did it from the bottom of your heart, with love. You did the best you could for her. And now your mother and father are at peace together. Be happy my love.' Sarah gave a little sigh and settled back in her seat, an aura of new-found peace surrounding her.

Secret: there is always hope for a resolution between loved ones, even after they have left the physical world.

For many of us, the fear of death in not so much about our *being* dead but about *how* we will die. Worries about our physical deterioration and appearance, about pain, panic or dying alone or in an institution can preoccupy our thoughts and prevent our coming to terms with death.

Moreover, when someone close dies an unnatural death, we not only mourn their loss but are forced to adjust to the unnatural way in which they died. It is a double blow: not only have they died, but the way they died appears to be senseless. Unnatural dying is abrupt and traumatic. There is no time for us to say our goodbyes.

It is easy to feel that much is lost when someone we love passes over. Especially hope. But I believe that every death we experience can be a positive opportunity to discover and learn more about ourselves. Yes, it's painful but many of life's greatest lessons are. I'm not saying don't grieve; I'm just saying that you should also look beyond your grief to realise you still have the essence of that person with you. They may not be there in body but they are still there all the same. Just as part of you is with them, part of them is in you. Do you want to betray that by giving up hope? I don't.

Boy in a Coma

There are occasions when our loved ones have not passed over but are poised between the physical and the spiritual world.

I looked at the expectant faces in the audience watching me. 'I have something very interesting here ... I believe it is someone who has a message for his mother. But he has not yet passed over.'

There was a surprised hush.

'It's a young man in hospital,' I continued. 'He's in a coma.'

From within the audience I watched as a woman slowly put up her hand. Lines of suffering were etched onto her brow.

'He says he knows he is between two worlds,' I told her. I heard the audience gasp. 'And he knows you're thinking about him.'

The woman nodded slowly.

'Right now he wants you to know he is watching home movies of all the family.'

'I don't know anything about that,' said the mother, looking puzzled.

'He wants you to know that he is still very much with you and is aware what's going on.' As I spoke, it transpired that the boy had been struck by lightning, which had left him in a vegetative state.

The boy's mother didn't say much in front of everyone there that day, so I wasn't sure if she believed in the connection or not. But when I caught up with her a few weeks later she confided that when she had got home later that evening, her daughter had told her she'd spent the afternoon in the hospital, watching home movies with her brother.

The rest of the world, the doctors and specialists, had told this family there was nothing of the boy's consciousness remaining and so the family had pretty much given up any hope of his recovery. But this message made them significantly change their attitude. It restored a glimmer of hope to them, not unrealistic hope that he would get better, but hope that he was still with them in some form. As his mother said: 'He is still our son and a brother in this family, and we will make every effort to talk to him in whatever way we can.' From that time on, they stopped talking about him in the third person when they were in the room with him.

When the time eventually comes for him to take his final breath, his family will perhaps be able to cope with their loss more easily, having taken their time to say their farewells.

Secret: there is always hope in some form, and even if it's just a small shining light, it is still worth having.

The Moth

I've always thought that the hurdles we face in life are there to make us become even smarter and stronger when we overcome them. The following parable makes the point perfectly:

A man found a cocoon of an emperor moth. He took it home so that he could watch the moth come out of the cocoon.

That day a small opening appeared in the cocoon and so he sat and watched the moth for several hours as the insect struggled to force its body through the tiny hole. Then the moth seemed to stop making any progress. It appeared as if it had gotten as far as it could and it could go no farther. It just seemed to be stuck.

The man, in his kindness, decided to help the moth, so he took a pair of scissors and snipped off the remaining bit of the cocoon. The moth then emerged easily. But it had a swollen body and small, shrivelled wings.

The man continued to watch the moth because he expected that, at any moment, the wings would enlarge and expand to be able to support the body, which would contract in time. Neither happened!

In fact, the little moth spent the rest of its life crawling around with a swollen body and small, shrivelled wings. It never was able to fly.

What the man in his kindness and haste did not understand was that the restricting cocoon and the struggle required for the moth to get through the tiny opening was the way of forcing fluid from the body of the moth into its wings so that it would be ready for flight once it achieved its freedom from the cocoon.

Freedom and flight would only come after the struggle. By depriving the moth of a struggle, he had accidentally deprived the moth of health.

Sometimes struggles are exactly what we need in our life.

If we were to go through our life without any obstacles, we would be crippled. We would not be as strong as we could have been.

Give every opportunity a chance.

Going for Your Dream

Let me tell you a story about a bloke called Steve. Steve came to see me about six years ago with his mother for a private reading. He was an affable chap, one of those people whose sincerity you feel straight away. His energy was warm and he immediately extended his hand towards mine. Usually when people come to see me privately they are somewhat wary, but with Steve I felt I already knew him. I should add that his mother was a lovely lady and shared the same characteristics as well.

I felt that Steve had incredible energy and told him so.

'Thank you,' he said politely.

'I'm getting a very interesting image, Steve. I have got a gentleman with me. He's putting an image in my mind of what he looked like, and the only way I can describe him is that in earthly life he looked like a certain actor. Do you know of the actor Bob Hoskins?'

'Yes. He's one of my favourites actually.'

'He sort of looks a little bit like him; quite short, quite tubby, nose a little bit out of shape, nice old boy, that's the feeling I get about him. Have you been involved with something in the artistic field? I'm getting a very strong sense of that from this fellow.'

Steve said that, yes, he did have artistic inclinations.

'And you've put it aside and thought, "No, I'm not going to go any further with that." I don't know if it's the word "pop" or "art" I'm meant to be connecting to here, but I know I'm supposed to be connecting to one or other of these words, or both of them. But the feeling that he's giving me is that you've put something of an artistic nature on the back burner and it's a reluctant decision and a very difficult one.'

'Yes, it's very, very difficult,' Steve admitted regretfully.

'Now, I don't know how he connects to you through Mum or Dad but what I can say is that as he connects to me, he puts a hue in mind, a hue or light over Mum, all right? So I feel he must connect with you through Mum. He's saying something very insistently: "Don't give up on a dream for the sake of five thousand pounds."'

Steve's eyes widened. 'I understand exactly what he's saying.'

It turned out the man in question was Steve's adopted father, Trevor. His biological father had passed away in the months before Steve was born, so sadly Steve never actually knew him. According to Steve, when he was seven years old his adopted dad had started a relationship with his mum but had opened his heart to her little boy too, accepting Steve as his own child. He had no children of his own and he was a man who felt education was the key to everything. He was also a very fit man, a farmer, so it had been a tremendous shock when he died very suddenly at the age of fifty three. In the morning he'd been fine. Then he had got out of bed and almost immediately had a huge, fatal heart attack.

'I really miss him,' said Steve. 'Of course there're lots of fond memories and I often end up laughing when I think about some of the things he did. He was very much a larger than life character, certainly someone that you wouldn't miss in a crowd. Small in stature but big in personality.'

'He's saying that if you have the will and desire then not having that £5000 should not stop you at all,' I explained. 'You can find a way if you want to.'

'Yes, I've been struggling with that for some time. There have been options but I just couldn't make it work for me.' It turned out that Steve was passionate about wanting to study drama but couldn't find a course he could afford. A lot of the courses cost around £5000 – an awful lot of money to find. He'd decided to keep looking for something he could afford and postpone his dream for a while.

Something else came to me: 'I'm getting the impression that Mum put aside a dream many years ago too because there just wasn't the money at the time.'

'I had no idea about that,' Steve said, surprised.

'And he doesn't want to see you do the same,' I continued. 'He says, "You might not reach the stars, son, but you can go a long way."'

'Yes.'

'You understand that he wants you to do it and not give up?'

'Yes, I do.'

At point Steve's mother joined in: 'I always wanted to act; it wasn't so much a matter of finances though in my case; it was very much that I think Trevor would've rather I'd gone walking the streets and selling my body to strangers than put myself on the stage! It wasn't a respectable profession, so I put it on the back burner, because I knew that he would never ever accept it. So it's interesting that he chose to come through and tell Steve to go for it. It seems that he's obviously seen a different side of things now.'

I continued with Trevor's message for his adopted son: '"You might not reach the stars, son, but you can go a long way." That's what he keeps telling you.'

'Mum has a saying which is "aim for the moon – even if you miss you will still end up among the stars", which is one of my favourite expressions, because drama is where I want to go, so that's where I'm aiming,' said Steve. 'From now on I'm aiming for the moon, so fingers crossed I'll end up around there somewhere!'

His mother added, 'I'm delighted to think that Trevor's keeping an eye on Steve too, and that he's recognised where he wants to be. With the encouragement that he's been given, I think he would be very foolish if he lets anything stand in his way. I only wish I'd had that encouragement myself. It's more valuable than any amount of money.'

It seemed that in the afterlife Trevor had realised the error of his ways in blocking the dreams of others and was trying to make amends, ensuring that nothing stood in the way of his adopted son Steve's happiness.

Secret: we should go for our dreams and have faith in our ability to do so. Our unseen loved ones will walk with us as our dreams unfold.

When people come to me for readings or join the audience for my shows, many of them are hoping for a communication from the afterlife that will answer their questions; that will give them hope, give them peace, show them the way and help make their decisions for them. They may even be hoping to find or hear something miraculous from the afterlife, although they have no idea what exactly that particular something is. When I stand in the middle of the stage, under the studio lights, it feels very humbling to look out at a sea of expectant, troubled, frightened and, yes, sceptical faces. I feel a big responsibility because I know that many of these people are waiting for something that might give them an answer, help them get on with their lives or give them an indication of something better on the horizon.

Sometimes it happens; a situation arises that is exactly as they would have wanted it. Someone who has passed over will decide to communicate and it will be the communication that friends or relatives need or have wished for. There will be a resolution and they will go away feeling happy or perhaps momentarily sad, but more content on the whole. People often ask me, 'Why do spirits say such insignificant, everyday things? Why don't they speak to us in a deep and meaningful way about the big things in life?' Well, the answer is that spirits are personalities and they will convey things that seem trivial in order to identify themselves. And sometimes that is all that's needed.

The Last Sigh

'Come on then, try and show me where you want to go – where are you?' I concentrated under the stage lights, a sea of pale faces watching me intently in the dark beyond. The connection strengthened: 'OK, my love, would someone please understand about Mum passing out of this life, and her last breath was almost like she was taking a sigh of relief?

'Can you understand that, my darling? About Mum passing from this life, and as she let go from this life, it was almost like she was sighing.' I was looking at a woman in the audience who was nodding in response.

I discovered that her name was Erica and she'd come along to the studio hoping she might receive a communication from her late mother. As I relayed the communication to her, she said, 'Always when I've talked of my mum passing, that is the most prominent thing; the sigh. Just the length of that sigh was quite frightening. We literally just watched her just empty her lungs. It was like this: "Huhhhhhh."'

'Does Mum have a sister?' I wondered.

Erica nodded.

'This side of life? OK. She wants to start off by saying will you let her sister know that everything is all right now? I'm not talking about an argument,' I explained, 'because this is not an argument; this was something between her and her sister, where they didn't quite agree with one another.'

'Yes.' Erica knew what I was talking about. 'I did know there was a disagreement before she died', she said.

'It was actually about her jewellery,' I explained. 'And I know that your aunt was deeply, deeply hurt by what was said and that none of it was true, not a smidgen! She had been accused of taking some, but it turned out your mum had actually hidden it. Then she had got a bit confused and forgotten. The problem is your aunt remembers the way your mum accused her and feels very hard done by. But she wants to make sure that you'll let her sister know that everything is all right now.'

'I will,' said Erica. 'Mum was the sort of person who'd say "I'm talking, and you will listen because I know best." She was just that sort of person; she liked the floor to be hers, in any circumstances she wanted to be at the forefront of everything.'

I continued: 'The impression I'm getting is that she's very relaxed about what you decide to do with the jewellery. She's saying, "Whatever you decide will be all right by me. As long as it stays in our family." And she wants to speak to her grandson.'

I turned to the person next to her. 'You, sir. Are you the lady's grandson?' A young man, well dressed but squirming a little uncomfortably in his seat, indicated he was.

'There's something she's observing in your life, so she's swung me over to you and she's said, "Tell him his ideas will be no good unless he can get them down on paper."' That wasn't quite it so I paused and went back to the connection: 'No, you don't mean paper, do you my love? – is that the only way you can understand it? Right, OK, I

think I know what you mean, but show me a picture ...
Now we have it. Would you please understand that you've
got to get something down on a CD? Have you got to do
something on CD?'

'Yes.' The young man gave a small frown and nodded
solemnly.

'OK. She's saying that you've got to get it on that silver
disk, or it will never go anywhere. And you look very calm
now, but your gran is also saying, "Will you please try and
do something about your temper? You don't get your point
across any better by continually losing your temper." All
right?

'I can't believe it!' interrupted Erica, clearly shocked by
the message. 'It's incredible she knows that!'

'It's only been in the last five months that you've kept
losing your rag,' I explained. 'Can you understand that? All
right – don't do it. She's saying, "Don't do it, it's not you –
you're not really like that."'

The youth was looking even more uncomfortable now,
shifting his weight from hip to hip in the seat and looking
everywhere around the theatre but at me. I wondered if
this was too much for him: 'Are you OK? I always say to
people I can stop at any time.'

'No, carry on, it's fine,' he mumbled.

'Do you know what she's talking about?'

'I've been in a recording studio recently, and I've been
trying to make my own CD with my friend. In my head
at the moment, I've been thinking about really wanting to
do it on my own. Although I've been thinking about it all

the time, I just haven't got down to doing it yet, so – yeah – she's just hit the nail on the head with that.'

'Will you do something about your temper?' I said. 'She's very clear on that.'

The young man gave me a sober look. 'I'm not a very angry person; I'm quite calm and generally I'm quite a good guy, but a couple of weeks ago, because I think I've been stressed with work and everything, I had quite a big outburst, where I upset the family. It really was a big one, and I've never let it affect me like that before. And it's only recently where I've been so stressed out that my temper has just gone through the roof.'

'You also didn't go on a holiday this year that you were invited on,' I noted.

'Goodness!' said Erica.

'Yes, you understand this? But the holiday did happen, you just didn't go, which all turned out well in the end because those boys were pretty bad news. Now she's saying, "Aren't you glad you didn't go?" She's saying that she doesn't want her grandson mixing with bad boys! Do you understand what Gran means?'

The lad shifted in his seat again. 'A lot of my friends had gone on the first group holiday, as friends, where they were going to somewhere like Ibiza, and I was really disappointed I couldn't go. And some of the crowd there weren't really friends, more like people I just hung out with. And it turns out, when they got back from holiday, that they got into quite a bit of trouble while they were out there so it was probably better that I didn't go,' he admitted.

'OK, darling, I'll tell her.' I turned again to Erica. 'She's just brought me back over to you, Erica, and is saying, "I went the way I wanted to, with a smile on my face, and I went where I wanted to be, and you made it all possible." You fulfilled her wish at the end. She's saying you moved heaven and earth to do it, because it was difficult, but she said, "You let me go in the way I wanted to go and where I wanted to be." It's her day to come and give her love to you and her grandson.

Erica swallowed back her tears, and explained that her mother had developed breast cancer but kept her condition a secret for a long time. Then she had made the choice not to have any treatment at all: 'She wanted to go because from the day my Dad died – they were best friends as well – she didn't want to go on living. She made it very clear that she always said that if she had a way out, she would choose to go, and that was her way.'

But it was clear to me that, although she had passed on from earthly life, she was still very much present in the life of her family, watching over them and caring for them all.

Secret: sometimes our loved ones are happy to leave this earthly world for one where they can be at peace and free from the ravages of time. We must be happy to let them go and begin the next stage of their spirit life.

I adore my parents and am fortunate to have a good relationship with them. Like all parents they had their own particular hopes for me, but nothing too ambitious: they hoped I'd do well at school, get a good job, meet a girl, get married and have children. All in all it was pretty simple stuff, really. The reality of my life is quite different. I didn't do well at school; in fact I hated the whole experience and was glad to leave at the age of sixteen.

They had to accept me as I was. But if they hadn't done so, what would I have done? What *could* I have done? I would've just had to follow my path, be true to myself and hope that they would eventually understand. Perhaps they themselves realised that they didn't fulfil the dreams of their own families in some ways.

We all need to find a balance of saying what we think but not letting our expectations spill over so much that they distress the person we love and destabilise them. It is a tough balancing act. Your hopes for a friend, say, to be reliable when it's just not in his or her character is not very realistic. Do you love your friends for what you see in them, for being someone who adds to your life or do you constantly want them to be something else?

Tim's Search for Himself

Since I began doing the *6ixth Sense* I've had little time to undertake private sittings, so much so I've virtually stopped doing them now. However, one that sticks out in my memory involves a man called Tim.

It was a pleasant spring day, one of the first of the year, and I remember I'd been able to open up all the windows in the house without freezing the place out!

My visitor was about thirty years old, wearing a smart well-tailored suit. By the way he looked down when he spoke I guessed he was shy by nature, so I thought it best to speak in a quiet and gentle manner with him. (Being extroverted by nature, over the years I've become used to toning myself down as there are many people who can find my energy intimidating and the experience of communicating with loved ones is often overwhelming enough in itself.)

He began by saying, 'You know I would never have dreamed of seeing a medium once upon a time. But I need to hear from someone I have lost before I can make an important decision in my life.'

I explained to Tim that I could never guarantee that any one person would be able to make a connection and it was best he did not tell me any more about why he had come as I did not want him to ruin his own sitting by telling me more than I needed to know.

I started to sense the presence of a gentleman who had been in his early sixties when he passed away. I began to explain to Tim that I had a sense this man was his father, who always gave the outward appearance of being rather stern and abrupt. But once you got to know him he was in fact a kind and intelligent man who enjoyed long, rambling conversations and who would always offer an opinion on all matters. He could be very narrow and fixed on certain subjects and the name 'Norman' seemed to fit him well.

'Yes, my dad's name was Norman and he was sixty-three when he passed,' Tim said.

As Norman began to strengthen his connection to me I was filled with the sense that he wanted to talk to his son about a matter that would have provoked many angry words between them when he was alive. I then had one of the most unusual clairvoyant experiences I think I have ever had. As I looked at Tim, he was surrounded by items of women's clothing. It was bizarre!

It could have been very amusing were it not for the feelings I was getting from Norman about his son: 'I sense your father is trying to communicate with you about how you perceive your gender identity.'

It was at this point Tim began to cry. 'Please tell my dad I'm so sorry, but I can't go on living like this,' he sobbed.

'"You must do what makes you happy," Norman says. "It's not important whether I completely understand or not."'

As the sitting progressed, a story began to unfold of how Tim had been secretly cross-dressing since his teens. Over time he had become increasingly aware that he was a woman trapped in a man's body. Recently he'd started gender reassignment counselling with the intention of eventually having surgery to become a woman. Before this could happen he was required to permanently put his male identity to one side and adopt his new female identity so he could live as a female. The rest of his family had been made aware of this and had generally been supportive.

However, before he passed, Norman had made it clear he did not understand transsexuals and thought them against the natural order of things. Tim was feeling guilty and hoped Norman could forgive him now for doing what he felt he had no control over.

I gathered he'd been aware of his true feelings for a long time.

'Yes I have, but I don't want to disappoint anyone, especially my father,' Tim admitted.

'Norman says he doesn't want you living half a life. Even though he does not understand, he cannot stand to see you unhappy.'

Tim nodded. There was no real joy in his reaction because it seemed as if he had exhausted himself worrying. It would have been better if he'd been able to gather his courage earlier and spare himself all those years of internal conflict. Yet sometimes we need that little signal. And sometimes we have to be the ones who give it to ourselves.

I think one of the many things we can learn from Tim's communication is that some things, in relation to who and what we are, are not a matter of choice, though how we deal with them always is. I can understand Tim feeling guilty but I also think that it is up to others to adapt to his right to choose his life. If you're in a situation where someone comes to you and tells you something as momentous as Tim had to tell his family, it's important to appreciate that they are surrendering their honesty to you. You may not initially be able to offer your understanding but you can still offer your love. From that understanding will grow.

I was so pleased that Norman came through and offered his love to his son, soon to be his daughter, even though he could not completely understand the reasons for Tim's choices.

Secret: we need not stand in the way of another's happiness even if we disagree with their choices. We need to accept their dreams just as they accept ours. Passing to the other side of life often allows the spirit to see that if we love someone we have to support their life decisions, even if we do not completely understand those decisions.

The Water Bearer

I want to share this parable with you because I think it relates to many situations we find ourselves in where we make life hard on ourselves, perhaps unnecessarily.

A water bearer had two large pots, one hung on each end of a pole which he carried across his neck. One of the pots had a crack in it, while the other pot was perfect and always delivered a full portion of water.

At the end of the long walk from the stream to the Master's house, the cracked pot always arrived only half full. For two years this went on daily, with the bearer delivering only one and a half pots full of water to his master's house. Of course, the perfect pot was proud of its accomplishments, fulfilled in the design for which it was made. But the poor cracked pot was ashamed of its own imperfection, and miserable that it was unable to accomplish what it had been made to do.

After two years of enduring this bitter shame, the pot spoke to the water bearer one day by the stream. 'I'm ashamed of myself and I apologise to you.'

'Why?' asked the bearer. 'What have you to be ashamed of?'

'I have been able, for these past two years, to deliver only half my load because this crack in my side causes water to leak out all the way back to your master's house. Because of my flaws, you have to do all of this work, and you don't get full value from your efforts,' the pot said.

The water bearer felt sorry for the old cracked pot, and in his compassion he said, 'As we return to the Master's house, I want you to notice the beautiful flowers along the path.' Indeed, as they went up the hill, the old cracked pot took notice of the sun warming the beautiful wild flowers on the side of the path, and was cheered somewhat. But at the end of the trail, it still felt the old shame because it had leaked out half its load, and so again the pot apologised to the bearer for its failure.

The bearer said to the pot, 'Did you not notice that there were flowers only on your side of the path, and not on the other pot's side? That's because I have always known about your flaw, and I took advantage of it. I planted flower seeds on your side of the path, and every day while we've walked back from the stream, you've watered them. For two years I have been able to pick these beautiful flowers to decorate my master's table. Without you being just the way you are, he would not have this beauty to grace his house.'

A Grandfather Watches Over

We'd had a very lively studio show in which we'd experienced it all: laughter, tears and all sorts of emotions flowing through what is essentially quite an impersonal space. Now I was getting the sense of a man standing between two women: 'There's an older male figure who draws an older and a younger woman together…'

A young woman put up her hand.

'Hello my love, is that your mother next to you?'

'Yes. I'm Catherine and my mother's Joan,' she replied.

'And your dad is in the spirit?' I wondered, though I already knew that wasn't quite it.

'Umm no … but …' she glanced towards her mother for reassurance, who laid a hand on her arm.

'Your grandfather.'

'Yes.'

'Darling, I'm not going to beat around the bush with you because I don't think your grandad wants me to: did you try to top yourself? It seems you did. Your grandad is just saying to me, "I'd have put you back every bloody time." Because your grandad doesn't muck about when he wants to say what's on his mind. He's very angry, but not with you. There is nobody, *nobody*, worth making you feel like this.'

Catherine cast down her gaze. 'I know that now.'

'You attempted suicide.'

She swallowed and then confessed, 'I was living away from home and I didn't think life was worth living and so one thing led to another. I couldn't see any way out, basically. I thought about ending it all, but I didn't have the guts to do it and when I was given the option to go back and live with my parents, I went home and my life has changed from then.'

'He's very angry, but not with you. He hopes you understand that.'

She understood perfectly. 'I'll take it as support and I'll bear that in mind for the future. The life I lead now is completely different and I'm glad he's there for me.'

'All right, he's saying promise that you will never think, let alone do something like that ever again,' I said sternly.

'I promise. I really do,' she said softly.

'Despite the fact that he was really tough when he first came through, your grandad's very proud that you've got your life back together again. I'm going to leave your grandad's love with you. Everything he's said today is to show you that he's aware of what's going on. And now you've got yourself sorted and that's all he's interested in. I'll leave his love with you, darling.'

Catherine replied, 'It makes me feel good because I know that my life all those years ago was wrong. My dad even refers to it as "my time away", and my life is really different; I'm all settled, I've got two lovely daughters and a lovely husband and it's just so much different to what it was all those years ago, and I'm proud of myself and I'm glad grandad is too.'

Later, after the show, Catherine told me that the communication had made her feel a bit warmer about the other side and what was waiting, as well as about her place in this life.

Secret:  no matter what we think of ourselves, we have an important role to play and should never underestimate our value. From where we stand, we often do not see the bigger picture, so we must trust that there is one and that we are a part of it. Ending our earthly life by our own hand only makes the journey more difficult.

Hope sounds like something that should be natural, within us all. But the truth is you have to work at it: you have to work at your optimism even when you're not sure where it's going. You have to be prepared to work for your dreams and hopes every day. You have to avoid those who would get in your way – negative voices, your historic knowledge of yourself and occasionally practicalities. It's incredible when you talk to people and realise that so many of us out there are suppressing our ambitions and goals because of other people and what they think. I know how it is: I had to go through quite a few unsatisfactory jobs and some good ones before I decided to take the plunge and develop my medium potential. But I knew I needed to let my spirit run free. And I feel deeply privileged that letting my spirit run free in my work as a spiritual medium has touched the lives of so many other people over the years.

We need to remember that we may have obligations to others but at the same time we have obligations to ourselves. If we don't fulfil these then we really are no good to other people. Sometimes we need to give something extra to ourselves first, and then fulfilling our hopes for others will follow naturally.

However, at times it can be particularly difficult to give ourselves the space we need, especially when we are caught up with the demands of our families. Illness and death can lead to huge divisions in families if communication breaks down and we feel we don't have the support or understanding we need. We need to keep talking and working together to get through difficult times. Virtually everyone knows of someone who has been involved in a family feud. These usually happen when someone feels that events have not gone their way and the situation is unfair. It's always harder in families because I think there is this assumption that because we are family we're all supposed to get on well. Well we're also human so happy families can sometimes be a bit of a tall order. Because of various pressures, arguments in families can last for years and even be passed on down through generations, cutting a huge divide. You know the sort of thing: 'Oh, I haven't seen my brother in forty years. He's just not like me and we stopped talking.' Or the aunt that nobody talks about because of something terrible she once did – though no one can really remember when it was, or even what it was.

You know the saying, 'The sins of the father are visited upon his sons.' If there is bad feeling in a family and it is not resolved, that feeling will seep down into the following generations. Believe me, I've seen it so often in the course of my work. It breaks my heart to see families who remain wounded by past events. There is no trust between people and even having the most basic relationship is not possible. And inevitably most conversations end up sounding like this: 'There is no way I will talk to her again unless she apologises.'

Secret: we are always in a position to make things better, no matter how negative a situation looks.

Pictures

As a medium it's not unusual to get the impression of photographs in your head. On this occasion I wasn't just seeing one or two. I was seeing hundreds of them and they were everywhere. I looked at a row in the audience and said: 'I'm settling around here somewhere; lots and lots and lots of photographs.'

A woman in her mid thirties, very petite with straight brown hair, put her hand up. She told me her name was Yvonne. 'It's so true, my flat is full of photos; there are photos on the fridge, there are photos on my boiler, there are photos everywhere; on the walls, the cabinets, just everywhere,' she said.

'Right, OK, well as long as you know we're going with this...' I cleared my throat and said gently, 'Did you have a little boy who passed into the spirit?'

She looked at me sadly. 'Well, I wouldn't know for sure if it was a boy or a girl; I couldn't go through with the pregnancy. In my heart I always thought a boy. But I never knew for sure.'

'I'm so sorry, my love, that your child was never identified to you as being a boy or a girl,' I said quietly, before moving on: 'What's the matter with Gran at the moment?'

'My grandmother?' She looked puzzled.

'No – *his* grandmother.'

'She has a lot of issues she's got to deal with, a lot of guilt.' Yvonne looked down at her hands, clasped in her lap.

'Oh darling, all right. And there is someone who's got to learn to forgive...'

'My mother,' Yvonne confided.

'I've got a little boy here and he's settling in front of you, and he's just telling me, "Granny's not right" or "Granny's not well". My love, there's never been good relationships between the females in the family, has there?'

'Nope.'

'But you're changing that.'

'Yes – yes,' she said with real energy.

'Right, OK,' I continued. 'Who is the younger girl who's telling you to do what you want to do, even though everyone else is saying don't?'

'That'll be my daughter.'

'Your son, her brother, is saying absolutely. He is in agreement. I feel as though there is an older female figure who connects to you and Mum. This poor woman feels guilty that she didn't do right by your mum, and your mum hasn't done right by you.'

'Hmm. My grandmother, I'm sure of it.'

'She knows what it's like to be burdened with guilt,' I observed.

Yvonne replied, 'My grandmother told me the day before she died that she'd had a bad marriage and she'd felt a lot of guilt, and I know that was passed on to my mother. My mother and I have a bit, like, locked horns, in the last year in particular. And every time I feel knocked back I try again, and I constantly look for the good in people, and I feel my mother needs to be able to forgive and then concentrate on the good aspects of people, and not the bad.'

'And she's feeling guilty about this,' I said. 'And she's told the little boy to say that thankfully you're breaking the chain. But don't give up on your mum.'

'I haven't,' she assured me.

'Keep trying.'

'I'm trying all the time.'

'Because the older lady, your grandmother, knows what it's like to pass over with guilt.'

'Yes, I know, that's why I'm working on my mum.'

'OK, keep plugging at it; you must be doing quite a good job. I'm going to leave your son and your grandmother's love and gratitude with you – it's good that you're doing something to break the chain.'

I felt admiration for this woman who was clearly determined not to repeat the mistakes of the past, even though she had suffered so much herself.

 Secret: the story of our lives is not pre-written and we have the power to rewrite it.

You may have read the following piece before – it is very well known. It's from *A Return to Love* by Marianne Williamson, and I think it is a very good reminder of our value and place in this world:

> Our deepest fear is not that we are inadequate. Our deepest fear is that we are powerful beyond measure. It is our light, not our darkness, that most frightens us. We ask ourselves, who am I to be brilliant, gorgeous, talented and fabulous?
>
> Actually, who are you not to be?
>
> You are a child of God. Your playing small doesn't serve the world. There's nothing enlightened about shrinking so that other people won't feel insecure around you.
>
> We were born to make and manifest the glory of God that is within us. It's not just in some of us; it's in everyone. And as we let our own light shine, we unconsciously give

other people permission to do the same. As we are liberated from our own fear, our presence automatically liberates others.

We can all make a difference. We do not need to repeat the mistakes of the past. We are not cogs caught up in a machine. There is so much more to us than that – we have the gift of hope to help us forward and we are not just physical beings: we have a connection with spirit.

3 | Secrets of Spirit

I BELIEVE we are all spiritual beings and that a way to express this is through knowing ourselves and finding a peace that comes from within rather than from the outside world. In my opinion, our spiritual learnings and practice can take many forms and should be intensely personal. However, I quite often find that people associate the idea of living a 'spiritual life' with particular beliefs. Some people choose to relate their spirituality to a deity whereas others seek it outside established religions. To my mind, it doesn't matter if eventually it leads us to a place where we can practise compassion, kindness and tolerance.

And here is where it takes real effort. Developing a way of living so that we can conduct our relationships with our family, friends and colleagues in a respectful and thoughtful manner means we need to acquire self-knowledge. Our spirituality should not be something that cuts us off from other people but instead brings us closer to them and creates stronger and more durable ties. Spiritual life is something we share. Remember, we're all part of a network of relationships, even if they are less than ideal.

As a spiritual medium I am perhaps more aware of that network than most, and how it extends beyond this earthly plane. Even though I've been a spiritual medium for many years I know that I will be forever answering the queries of sceptics as long as I do the work I do. But that's OK. People have as much right to be sceptical of spiritual mediums just as they did of, say, Galileo when he attempted to persuade scientists and clergy of the early seventeenth century to look through his telescope to see the proof that Copernicus was right: the sun really was at the centre of a system and it was surrounded by revolving planets. Back then he was greeted with ridicule and many even refused to look through the telescope.

Today we smile at the ignorance of Galileo's mockers: 'How could they not have seen the obvious?' we ask. Now, any schoolchild knows that the sun is at the centre of a solar system with Earth as just one of nine planets orbiting it. However, I think it's the same situation with the work that I and other spiritual mediums do. The idea that there is some form of life after death is – and will probably continue to be – the subject of much debate.

I can only say that we are not only physical matter, but also spiritual essence. Think of yourself as a spiritual being in possession of a physical body. Watch the process of nature of death, rebirth and renewal and you will see how existence continues even beyond this thing called death. In the same way that we learn to understand the physical world with our physical senses (sight, hearing, taste, touch and smell) so the afterlife can be felt by a set of spiritual senses.

The man in the next story is interesting because I think he wanted to believe, but he was fighting against it.

The Doctor's Affair

I remember meeting a rather urbane and confident doctor once. I later discovered that he had taken part in a discussion about life after death in which a group of medics had talked about what they'd observed when people died. This doctor had proved quite stubborn about the possibility of life after death and had been rather vocal about his views. As a dare, one of the other doctors suggested that he raise the subject with me, so he came to see me.

I'm very fine-tuned to people's body language but in his case I didn't need to be: it was so obvious that he thought this was all a big joke. He walked through my hallway with a superior sort of swagger that said, 'Go on then, show me what you've got!' Honestly, he reminded me of a cowboy who was heading for a showdown. Still, I always say each to their own. Whether he would admit it to himself or not, he had come for a service and – whether or not he was cynical – I was here to provide it. It might even be fun.

So I invited him to sit down and he lowered himself into the chair in the reluctant manner of someone who passionately wished he was not there; in fact he looked as though he would have preferred to be just about anywhere else. In situations like this I don't feel any need to go out of my way to convince someone that the experience they are about to have will be an authentic one. I believe people should make up their own minds about it and am secure enough in myself not to have to push the truth on them.

Although we hadn't really talked I became aware of a connection that concerned him. 'Your mother, she had a strange middle name, didn't she?' I asked.

He narrowed his eyes. 'Specifically what do you mean by a strange name?'

'Just a moment.' I paused. 'It's coming to me. Yes, I'm getting something starting with Z...Zelda.'

Well, I have never seen someone's expression change so fast. 'Nobody knows my mother's middle name is Zelda,' he blurted. He had shifted from leaning back in his chair to leaning forward. He was listening and now he was definitely interested in what I had to say.

I saw no point in beating about the bush: 'Your mother is telling me she's incredibly upset about the way you've treated Marian. In fact she thinks your behaviour has been atrocious.'

This comment seemed to jolt him. His face changed expression yet again and I could see I had really hit a nerve, if not several.

'Can you tell me what else she is saying?' he asked, almost as if he were a little boy in the headmaster's office.

'Well, I can tell you she's disgusted about the business with Catherine. She feels that you have been unfair to Marian and you're potentially going to ruin, even devastate, two people's lives,' I explained.

He was visibly shaken. There was no mistaking that he had been taken off-guard. There was a moment before he spoke: 'She's talking about the affair I've been having for the past eighteen months. Catherine's the nurse I've become involved with. Marian's my wife. I don't think Marian knows, but our life together hasn't been all that great since it began.'

'Your mother is very clearly voicing her displeasure,' I said frankly.

He nodded slowly.

I continued, 'She wants me to tell you, "Son, I may love you but I don't actually like what you're doing right now and you need to know that."' In fact, his mother was telling him off for being so thoughtless and self-centred, and for potentially destroying both women's lives through his selfishness. She evidently thought he should have known better and I imagine she felt she had a right to expect more from her son.

What she did at that moment was something we often find hard to do with the ones we love. She delivered hard medicine in a totally honest way. The fact that she told him this from her place in the spirit world demonstrates that death does not change the way people feel about us. What we do and the way we behave will still impact upon them and we need to remember that.

 **Secret:** those who taught you and guided you when you were young are still interested in you when they have passed over. So behave in a way that makes them proud.

The Hiding Place

The following is a Sioux Indian story, one of many from Native American Indian folklore. I think it is very positive and has meaning for us all, especially in difficult and tragic times:

The Creator gathered all of Creation and said, 'I want to hide something from the humans until they are ready for it. It is the realisation that they create their own reality.'

The eagle said, 'Give it to me; I will take it to the moon.'

The Creator said, 'No. One day they will go there and find it.'

The salmon said, 'I will bury it on the bottom of the ocean.'

'No. They will go there too,' the Creator replied.

The buffalo said, 'I will bury it on the Great Plains.'

The Creator sighed, 'They will cut into the skin of the Earth and find it even there.'

Grandmother Mole, who lives in the breast of Mother Earth, and who has no physical eyes but sees with spiritual eyes, said, 'Put it inside of them.'

And the Creator said, 'It is done.'

The spiritual tradition that for me represents faith teaches the basic foundations of human relationships: not to kill others, cause others harm, humiliate others, or jeopardise their welfare. That is, we need to control ourselves enough not to cause injury. It also teaches practices that help us accept our neighbours: tolerance, patience, gentleness and compassion.

The art of living a spiritual life is therefore expressed through our relationships. To love and to relate are the same thing; as our relationships become conscious, we become conscious of love. The quality of our relationships shows the nature of that love.

When somebody we love or care for dies, it's not unusual for our emotions of grief to extend into our relationship with God. In the pain and loneliness inherent in our loss, it may seem that God is far away. Past comfort and feelings of having that faith can give way to emptiness, anxiety, and sadness. We have to go into the emptiness with bare faith, simply hanging on and trusting that what we have heard or been told is true. Faith does not take the pain of loss away or diminish our grief but it does help us to live with the difficult emotional process as we move slowly toward healing.

Knowing how we should prepare for the loss of a loved one is one of life's most challenging situations. It is perhaps one of the most 'out of our control' experiences that we will ever face. Death always comes unexpectedly, whether we are ready or not. And it comes in many different ways. There is not just our own death we have to face but those of the people we love. When our mother or father dies, when our son, husband or anyone close to us dies, that is also like a death to us. They have been an important and core part of our being, and when someone we love dies, a part of us also dies. So it's not only in our own death that death comes; whenever anyone we love dies, death comes to us as well. And no matter how well prepared we are it can at times be very depressing and deeply overwhelming.

A Mother's Grief

Sometimes people ask me if I feel personally responsible for the people who come to me for readings. I'm aware they're placing a lot of hope in my hands and that is a responsibility of sorts. But as for me being responsible for their feelings, I'm afraid I'm not a superhuman – I'm just Colin. 'Do you feel it when someone is upset?' a journalist once asked me. Of course I do. I'm very aware, painfully aware in some cases, of the depths of despair that some people are in. But I have to remind myself I'm there to give the message.

On this occasion I sensed a youthful spirit trying to connect: 'I've got a young man connecting to me, and he's very intent on making it happen. I'm going to have to use a very ambiguous term here, but this is what he is putting through to me – that he wants to connect to his family here today.'

A woman looked at me and went to raise her hand.

'My love, have you got a young man who passed into the spirit and the circumstances aren't quite explained? He's giving me his name, Brendan, no – Bernard.'

She looked at me.

'My love, what's your name?'

'Elaine.'

'Elaine, I don't think it's necessarily with you, but I think it's one of the ladies in your family he wants to connect with. It's so important he gets this message across, because she has stopped believing and that's making it harder for her to accept the situation. He is saying she has lost her faith.'

'Yes.'

'Can you understand that?'

'Yes,' Elaine said quietly. 'I've been dealing with this for some time.'

'She has never forgiven herself because he went over and. Or God for that matter. She has said, "There cannot be a God because God would not do this to me!"'

'Yes, it's my mother.'

'All right, can you tell Mum to open the drawer up: "Get it out and hold it in your hand again, and get your faith back."'

'Yes.'

'Would you understand that there is a bi-annual or annual pilgrimage to Bernard's grave or his place of passing?'

Elaine nodded. 'Yes, there is.'

'He's saying, "Can we please stop this now?" He says it's

not necessary and it's making things worse for your mother, even though she doesn't realise it.'

At that moment, the man who was sitting alongside Elaine interrupted. 'I told you it wasn't doing any good and that you should put an end to it,' he said heatedly.

'He is very serious about this and he wants me to ensure that you understand this message is not half-hearted. He feels it serves no purpose at all to visit the grave in this ceremonial way.'

'Yes,' said Elaine, 'I understand.'

'All it keeps doing is reminding everyone that his life – his earthly life – was tragically cut short, and acting in this way won't bring him back.'

I paused for a moment before continuing: 'Do you remember the young lad a number of years ago who won *Opportunity Knocks*? His name was Neil something or other, and he sang a song called "Mother of Mine", and now Bernard's put that song in my mind and he's saying, "Will you take the thought of that song home and give it to Mum as my gift to her?"'

'Thank you, Colin,' Eileen replied. 'I can understand that. Bernard sang songs to my mother constantly. They were all songs about mothers, and he loved my mother dearly. He seemed to have this repertoire of songs that were all about mothers and he would serenade mum endlessly. And I know my mother really misses him.'

'I think Mum will understand what it means.'

Elaine explained what had happened. 'There're ten boys in my family, and Bernard and I were very close.

When he died in a car crash on 27 December he was only thirty-three. He had lived with me for about six months before that, here in London. He went back to Ireland and was supposed to come back in the New Year but the crash happened and that was the last I saw of Bernard.'

Eileen stopped and looked down at her hands, folded on her lap. 'He loved my mother very much. She has this picture of Bernard on her living room wall, and she'll sit and talk to it for hours. And I have to take the blame for that, because a couple of months ago I told her to take it down and put it away, because it wasn't doing her any good. But because of the way Bernard died, none of us could understand why God would take him away from us the way it happened. So since then, most of us have stopped going to church – it sounds a terrible thing to say – but we've all just gone our own separate ways.'

'You've lost your faith, haven't you?' I ventured.

'Yes, but I think I have to move on, because I think about him twenty-four hours of the day; I dream about him at night – I sometimes have not-so-nice dreams about him, which disturbs me, and I think now that he was here today that that will take it all away from me. I just hope and pray to God that he's in heaven.'

'He's saying, "Will you take the thought of that song home and give it to Mum as my gift to her?"'

'Yes, I most certainly will,' said Elaine. She seemed like she had taken the message very much to heart and wanted to make some changes.

'He also says, "You finally got to wear a ring that fits you..."'

'Well, Bernard always said that he'd like to see us married one day.' She gestured to the man next to her. 'We've been talking about it these past few days, so I think that's what he is getting at. Bernard thought a lot of John.'

John smiled. 'Me and Bernard were like brothers, really. When he was here we used to spend a lot of time together. We just hit it off from the outset. I drive a lorry for a living, and I do night shifts because I prefer to drive when there's less traffic. Bernard used to love coming out with me in the truck. But apart from that, when I wasn't working we'd be playing pool or drinking somewhere. You know, he was just a great man to be with, top man.'

John turned towards Elaine: 'For me personally, there is relief in the thought that Elaine will maybe let go now and find her faith again. Because before, she just couldn't and there would be tears to the point where it's very hard to take, just watching her in pain.' He leant over to her and kissed her gently on the brow.

 Secret: while we may question our faith after the passing of a loved one, it will always be there for us if we wish to return to it once more.

While religion and having a known faith can help some people in their lives, in my opinion formal religion isn't always necessary for inner peace. The power to believe in ourselves and in a more harmonious life for ourselves and the wider world lies within us all. That said, when we are feeling fragile an established faith may immediately give us something to hold on to. Nonetheless there are moments when our faith will be sorely tested, no matter how firm it is. It has happened to me when loved ones have died: it has made me question the fairness of life.

Spiritual transformation is always a process of birth–death–rebirth, until we eventually struggle to new life. Loss is naturally part of this. We may wish that we could run from it but we can't. What we can do is open ourselves to this unfolding process. We can trust that something new will follow our time of death and despair. This truth is at the heart of spiritual growth and development. The poet, Rumi, described it well when he wrote:

> From a worm's cocoon, silk.
> Be patient if you can, and from sour grapes will come
>   something sweet.

Reunited in Spirit

The death of children is always very moving; a child coming forward to give a communication to its parents will always reduce me tears. On this occasion I had the sense of someone's son – I wasn't sure what age – being involved in a blood transfusion. There was something about the kidneys not functioning and it all seemed very sad. It'd generally been a day when I'd received some very upbeat communications – I mean upbeat from the point of view that those who'd passed over had not died tragically. As soon as I felt this communication come through I knew it would be something quite different.

I took a step forward, put my hand up to shield me from a light that seemed to be in the wrong place, and asked, 'Would anyone here know about a son, possibly quite young, who had problems with his kidneys?'

A woman who I guessed was in her late thirties, put her hand up. She had a fair complexion with red hair, someone who could look rather striking if she chose to do so.

'Is that you, my love? What's you name?'

'Verity.'

'What an unusual name! Come a bit closer and we'll see if we can get a stronger connection.' I beckoned her over and the man next to her, who must've been her husband, stepped forward with her.

'It was your baby, my darling.'

'Yes,' said Verity. 'I had a baby whose kidneys stopped functioning and they gave him blood.'

'But he wasn't the only one, was he, Verity? Because I'm getting the impression of three in my mind.' The audience gasped.

Verity suddenly had the saddest, most tragic face I'd seen on anyone in a long time. 'I've actually lost three babies Colin,' she said in a small, lost voice.

Upon hearing this there was a kind of uncomfortable hush in the audience. My audiences have been present when the death of a child is discussed but to hear someone talk about losing three is very difficult for onlookers to cope with. It was up to me to pick things up in the most sensitive way I could and keep going.

'Verity, would you and your husband like to come on to this stage and sit on the sofa here?' I asked.

I watched them as they made their way towards the stage, this remarkable couple who had clearly been through so much. 'Here you go, sit down here. And have this.' I handed them each a glass of water. 'I feel that it's your respective grandmothers who are trying to piece this all together, to bring all the children together.'

Verity wiped her face with a tissue. 'OK,' she said, taking a sip.

'But the thing is, there's this little boy where nothing was spared; everything and anything was done to keep him on this side of life.'

'Yes, I understand that,' she said. Her husband put a protective arm around her and held her close.

'My love, from what both of your grandparents are showing me, I know that the issue was in the kidney and then they had a problem with the toxins building up in the liver.'

Verity nodded.

'But what your gran is showing me is that the inside of this little lad just wasn't developed properly.'

'No Colin, he wasn't.' Verity wiped a tear away and looked up towards the ceiling for a moment, before turning to face me again. 'He was born with problems.'

'Now, what's this about a handprint?' I questioned gently.

'We've got the handprint and footprints of our little baby boy.' She was doing her best to be very brave but it was me at this point who was going to cry. I had to try incredibly hard to keep the tears back so I could continue: 'All right now, there is a poem or some sort of rhyme you have written down.'

'We've, yes, we've...' As the tears began to flow, Verity struggled to find the words.

'Do you keep it with you all the time or near you?'

'Yes, yes, we do.'

At this point her husband joined in. He cleared his throat and said, 'We just feel it brings him closer.'

'Well, now when you get home, read the second line of the poem that's with the photograph. You know what I mean ... read the second line. It won't make sense of anything that has happened to you but it'll reinforce the fact that your son's been here with you today.'

'I think I understand,' said Verity.

'Good. Take comfort in the fact that all three of your children are being looked after by your respective grand-mothers. Please try to do that.'

There seemed little more that I or anyone else could say.

 Secret: we must not despair because we can't always see the big picture. Just recognise there is a big picture.

I try to live a spiritual life. I don't mean in the sense that I communicate with those who have passed over: that is my professional side. I mean that in all aspects of my day-to-day life I try to apply my own spirituality so that I and those that I love benefit. This means I try to approach life in a positive and accepting way, aware that just as my loved ones accept my flaws and mistakes, I too must take their own human characteristics and personality traits as a matter of course.

In the past few years we've seen a huge desire on the part of people to search for something more spiritual in their lives. All sorts of people – even those you wouldn't expect – have stepped out of their normal lives in the search for something more meaningful. For some that has meant reading books, for others it is searching for spiritual therapies – healing, meditation and especially yoga. Still others have decided to take their search even further and explore their newfound desire in Ashrams or retreats.

I'm not suggesting this is wrong in any way, but I meet many people who tell me they are into something 'spiritual' yet I don't really see evidence of that in their daily lives. They do their yoga or chanting or whatever once a week and then tell me how good they feel. But my question is always, 'How do you carry that into your daily life?' Are these people merely skimming the surface or, dare I ask, playing at their chosen practice? I say that because true spirituality is something we carry with us every day of our lives. We can't buy it and clip it on like a mobile phone cover when we feel we need a spiritual 'hit.' Likewise, we can't throw it away when it suits us. By all means go to the yoga class or do your meditation twice a week but don't kid yourself that those two hours or so will absolve you from being responsible for how you conduct yourself for the rest of the time!

We all have choices and we can all make those into spiritual choices. By that, I mean making choices that consider how our actions and their consequences can influence the lives of others. This doesn't mean that you have to be someone's lap dog, always pleasing them. Nobody should put off their own obligation to themselves just to make others feel better. But when you do what's right for you and harm nobody else in the process you are being true to yourself. And it is from there that your inner peace will come. Not from some outside influence.

Sometimes the greatest enemy of a free spirit can be logic and rationality. When we stop responding on an emotional, intuitive level, we miss out on the essence of life. Sure, daily life is largely about practical things, but don't be fooled: it's in our emotional responses that happiness lies.

I mentioned earlier in this book, when I was a child I began to experience intuitive impressions from about the age of ten. I suppose I assumed everyone did the same thing: as a child you don't think in such logical or rational terms. It was only when I was told that others did not feel or sense the same things that I realised this gift wasn't available to everyone. I never really understood how or why I was getting all this information at the time and of course as a child I didn't even question it. I think we could all benefit from adopting this innocent attitude: you may not be psychic but you can tap into your intuition. You just have to open up.

This next story demonstrates that intuition lies within us if we just learn how to listen to ourselves.

Trusting Your Intuition

I have a friend who dreamt about opening a business of her own. This had been her dream for many, many years and finally her opportunity arrived. This lady is an absolute go-getter and she was itching to find the right space to set up her office. She looked at loads of different places and finally found one that she thought would be perfect. Then she got cold feet. Just like that. The day before she was due to meet the estate agent to discuss the contract she suddenly froze. She told me later that she'd felt uneasy and started remembering the words of people who thought her enterprise wasn't a good idea.

When she called me to talk about it, my response was that it was perfectly normal to feel unsure about taking such an unfamiliar step, but that many, many people had done it before her and she was just as good as they were. But still she felt she just couldn't do it. She was toying with the idea of cancelling the meeting although she knew that if she did her moment would pass. I tried to reassure her, telling her she had to go with her gut feelings on this, before we said our goodbyes. Eventually I caught up with her a couple of weeks later.

'What happened?' I asked.

'Well, Colin, as you know I was so close to backing out of the whole thing and just burying my head in the sand. But then I remembered that my mum and dad, who have both passed, had brought me up to believe in myself and that I have always come through before,' she said. (I had once given her a communication from her parents, something I don't generally do with friends.)

She explained, 'How could I let them down now? More importantly, how could I let myself down? So I just decided I had to do it. Although I had some doubts and the negative words of all those people running round my mind, I just knew deep down that I had to make the most of this chance. In the end it was my own inner voice I had to listen to.'

'And you did it?'

'And I did it. And here I am.' She proudly turned the key in the door of her new premises.

This story is a classic example of what we all go through in moments of doubt. We tend to listen to the voices of others instead of trusting our own intuition. We fear making the wrong decision. But really there is no wrong decision if we make it ourselves.

Secret: if we trust our intuition we are very often doing what our loved ones in the afterlife would expect and want for us.

From day one in our lives we learn patterns of living: first through our parents and then later these extend into our immediate environment, and finally into the world. All these patterns of living are created and reinforced by family and friends, and by our religious, cultural, ethnic, educational, economic and political backgrounds. They all support and produce our beliefs, both the ones we adopt and the ones we create.

Ultimately all those beliefs project to the outside world and people see us as we see ourselves. If we believe we're unsuccessful and a loser then that is what people will think about us. The power of our own self-belief is very strong: who hasn't noticed an attractive but still rather ordinary-looking woman outshine one who is obviously a beauty? That's usually because the one who is not a world-class beauty has this aura of confidence about her that other people respond to.

These are some people who are blessed with enormous self-belief and have a strong sense of security in themselves. Sometimes it is just random, but in many cases it is their self-belief that makes things happen and I suppose that might even include communications from those who have passed.

Inspiration and a Warm Heart

It almost felt as though Belinda was a friend. I don't mean she was overly familiar but she had a wonderful aura about her. I felt that she'd enjoyed many happy moments in life and was not the sort of person to let anything worry her. There was something was quite spiritual about her. You could tell she listened, that she thought about things and was very kind and thoughtful to others.

She told me she was very hopeful that her grandmother would come through for her. She said that this remarkable woman had been instrumental in shaping her life. I was careful to tell her what I tell everyone: that if the spirit is ready it will come through and communicate. If it isn't then it won't.

It was a warm day so we had some fruit juice before we began. Sometimes when I open myself to the spirit world, the person who is being sought doesn't come through. Sometimes the lines are crossed. On this occasion I was getting a good connection but I couldn't quite work out the relationship of the female mother-figure to Belinda, but I pressed on regardless: 'Belinda, this is very interesting. I've got a name, a Patricia or Pat. The challenge I have is that although I know it's from the maternal side of your family, that is your mother's side, I am unclear as to whether Pat is your mother or grandmother.'

'Well, I know this is going to sound very odd,' Belinda smiled, 'but you're absolutely right. It's both of them.'

'Your grandmother was a much bigger part of your upbringing than your mother would have been. She was like your mother.' That much was clear.

Belinda explained that her grandmother had taken on both roles in her life: mother and grandmother. As we spoke, it became clear that there had been some confusion in her childhood; until the age of ten she had thought her grandmother was her mother and nobody had told her any different. Of course, being a child, she didn't ask questions. However, when her grandmother fell ill, she was packed off to London for a year to stay with a woman she thought was her aunt. In fact the woman she thought was her auntie was her mother.

We moved on. 'My love, I feel like we need to go back quite a long way here. Would you understand a child who burned themselves on a range or an iron?'

'Yes, that was me.'

'What my mind shows me, darling, is one of these old irons that heated on a stove or a range. I just have this strong sense of burning skin.'

'Yes. I was a bit naughty really,' Belinda admitted. 'Always putting myself where I shouldn't be.'

'But I'm being told you had been warned twice.'

'Well, I was pretty little…'

I continued: 'Your grandmother is saying to me that although she had accepted her responsibility for you and thought of you as her child, that incident had a huge impact on her and made her commit herself to the fact that she would look after you forever more.'

Belinda gave me a beautiful smile. 'I had a wonderful childhood; happy, comfortable, close and loving. It just proves, I think, that you don't need a conventional family setup to have a nourishing and warm family life. Grandmother and I had a very, very close relationship. We did everything together: went to the cinema, went out for meals, to the park, everywhere. I remember how she used to plait my hair with rags while she told me stories and sang songs. It was just one of those perfect old-fashioned cosy moments.

I knew she was telling the truth: 'Yes, she's telling me this and – I hope you can take this in the right vein because she thinks you can – she reluctantly took you when you were tiny, but was very glad that she did.'

Belinda told me that she understood exactly what her grandmother was saying and was in no way offended. 'That would fit in perfectly with what I've been told. I believe that she adopted me when I was six weeks old. I'm not exactly sure why and can only imagine that it was because of my mother not being married and religion or something. Of course this is only what I think, but I'm going to find out properly because I only have a birth certificate in her name.'

'She's asking me to tell you that, if it's still not too late to look into, there is a Canadian connection.'

'Really? Is she saying anymore about that because I'm not sure where to start,' Belinda wondered.

'I'm going to have to say Canada because she is showing me the maple leaf, which pretty well seals it.'

'Well now…Canada; that's interesting because obviously I'm going to try to trace who my father was. I suspect he's dead in any case, but with what I've heard at this reading I need to satisfy my curiosity. So obviously the question in my mind is whether or not my father went to Canada?'

I gently steered Belinda away from that line of enquiry because I was seeing a picture of her with her hair done in rather a posh way. In it, she seemed to be featured in a magazine photo. 'Was that you, Belinda?' I exclaimed, fascinated.

Belinda blushed, then admitted, 'I have done.'

'You were modelling!'

She nodded. 'It was in 1960 as I recall. I used to be a hair model and I was employed by Sassoon and various other people, so it was quite prestigious work. And I was involved in a hair competition; I think the hairdresser came second or third, which is why my picture was published. While we're on the subject I should tell you I got my picture in the paper twice: I was also in a skiffle group. I used to play drums and sing, and they put our photo in the paper.'

I laughed. 'Your grandma wants to say that she wouldn't have approved of it while she was still here, but watching it all happen she was very proud of you. She loves you dearly, with a passion. Her remorse is that she feels she should have told you more. She understands you must have questions and she hopes you can accept this from her: by not telling you she thought she was protecting you. She's saying if she'd ever thought that would cause you painful curiosity or the feeling of being unanchored to life, then she would have told you more.'

'That's so good to hear,' Belinda said thoughtfully. 'My grandmother died when I was about twelve years of age; at the time I was with my mother in London.

When she became ill I was very upset because my mother didn't tell me and she didn't even let me go to the funeral – she didn't even tell me.' The tears welled up in Belinda's eyes.

As Belinda's grandmother faded out from me and finished this rather lovely and warm communication there was one last thing to put through to Belinda: 'She loves you very, very much.'

Belinda thanked me and we chatted a bit more about the message. She told me that she'd been wanting to contact her grandmother for some time and wanted to know that the older lady was aware of how she'd grown up and the four wonderful children she had.

 Secret: the affection a loved one has for us does not die; it remains with us exactly as it has always been – a source of strength in difficult times.

Death is perhaps the most difficult of life's events to cope with, yet one that we prepare for and talk about very little. Imagine if it were just something we could get over quickly. We could get the news, go into shock for a bit, cry, get angry and then sit down and talk rationally about how our loved ones are now at peace. After that we'd go straight back to normal. By the end of the week we'd have accepted it all, understood it had to happen and find ourselves restored to calm...

But what makes us human is that our emotions are much more complex than that. We don't know what we will actually do. We'll feel most of the above to some extent or another, but our grief won't be so neatly organised, and it will come in waves that might seem out of proportion to what we 'should' be feeling. For example, it can be hard to accept that we feel really angry at the deceased, at ourselves, or even at God. Death can feel as though someone has stolen something precious from us without any good reason, especially when the loss concerns a young person's life.

The experience of grief is a multi-faceted one, bringing with it change, turmoil, and/or the loss of hopes and dreams. Grief is not something we readily acknowledge in our society. Yet it is often an important part of most life changes and experiences. Families who can acknowledge their grief and learn healthy ways to express their pain can then free their emotional energies to focus on life and the challenges ahead.

Grief over a lost child can be deep and unyielding. Some parents may continually look back and wonder what might have happened if that child had grown up, thus remaining stuck in the past. There are also those who take the spirit of that life and use it to make something positive happen in their lives, thus ensuring that child is remembered in a warm, loving way. They understand that somehow, in coming to grips with death they are developing a deeper appreciation of life.

Turning Loss into Positive Action

Way back in the early days of my television appearances I invited Jenny, Jonathan and their friend Amy to join me for what was to prove a truly emotional reading. It turned out that Jenny and Jonathan had lost their prematurely born son after only twenty-eight days. Eighteen months later I caught up with them again and discovered that their first visit to the show had had a major influence on their lives.

The story began when the couple discovered that Jenny was pregnant. One of the first to hear the good news was their close friend Amy. She told me the story: 'When Jenny and Jonathan announced the pregnancy, like any couple they were ecstatic, preparing for their new baby to be born. Then Julie gave birth prematurely and the hospital informed them their little baby was seriously ill. Then he died after just twenty-eight days, and it obviously hit them very hard. I don't think anyone can describe what they went through during that period; his death really affected them, and they began to look for answers but didn't get any, which left them in limbo.'

When I spoke to the couple about that initial reading, Julie told me how it felt to receive the communication at the time: 'For me, I thought this is an opportunity that's hopefully going to give us some comfort. And it was like a telephone link.'

At the time her husband had been more sceptical. As he put it: 'Whereas Julie is very spiritual, I tend to be more scientific. I wanted physical proof, if you like. But I went along to your show with a very open mind; I thought if this so-called afterlife is out there, it'd be good to see how it worked at first-hand. Then you asked us who Thomas was and we said he was a friend. But then we realised you weren't talking about that Thomas, who's alive – it was actually about our baby who had passed over.'

Both Jenny and Jonathan were over the moon when I told them that their baby was fine and being well-looked after by his grandmother in the spirit world.

Amy, who'd been very close to them right throughout that difficult time had observed how things had changed for this lovely couple: 'They've come on absolutely leaps and bounds since your show; it's almost like they've put what they'd been through behind them and can suddenly face the rest of their lives with a totally new perspective. They had tried to box away the past and tried to put it in a different place, but when they realised that Thomas had come through and that he was with a member of the family they felt they could continue with their future, incorporating him into it.'

'One of the things that occurred to me,' said Jonathan, 'was that our story would have a lot of relevance to other people and touch them because so many people have lost newborn babies. Of course it did and then people got in touch with us after that first show to share their own experiences, which helped us a lot. We just didn't feel cut off anymore.'

He continued, 'And really, that reading has changed the way I view life; I've learnt that you should keep an open mind. I feel now that, yes, my son is with me every day. That one particular reading has given me a great deal of comfort. Even if, say, there isn't an afterlife, at the end of the day, when I've died, if there isn't one I'm not going to know the difference anyway, am I? So it's made it much more comfortable to live.'

The people who got in touch after the show gave Jenny and Jonathan a new network of friends; they all shared the pain of losing a child through premature birth. But with their new positive outlook, they decided to use their own experience to help others.

Jenny told me: 'There're four sets of parents that have all got together to set up this support group called 24-Weeks Plus. Our aim is to support and help other parents who've been in our position. What we did find is when you're in a neo-natal unit it's very alien, and although the staff there are very good and supportive, sometimes you just need to speak to other parents who've actually been through the same kind of stress levels that you're going through at that moment. We've also found that people don't really want to speak to someone over the phone – especially strangers – so our support system is via email.

'If you wake up at two o'clock in the morning and you feel you need to talk to someone, at least you can just put your thoughts down and send the email. We do access the email box every day so we can guarantee a reply within 24 hours. Our long-term aim, along with the other parents we've met, is to extend the charity worldwide. It's going to be a struggle, but we're strong and we're going to fight on with that.'

 **Secret:** while death may be a sad and difficult time, if we choose to see it as a life-changing event in a positive way, it can herald a new start in life that is fulfilling.

Death can mark the birth of something new and wonderful. However, sometimes outside circumstances affect the grieving process and the responses of the bereaved. These may include the age of the deceased and the circumstances of death, whether the loss was sudden or expected, and the cause of death, particularly if violence was involved (such as suicide, disaster, crime). The nature and quality of the relationship between the deceased and the bereaved person is important, too. Earlier unresolved losses, whether occurring through death, divorce, or broken relationships may also complicate an individual's recovery.

At times, we may try to view our loss in as positive a light as possible, to be as spiritual about it as possible – 'it was meant to be', 'it was her time', 'it's all part of a greater pattern' – but if we find that we are still feeling bitter and trapped in our grief than perhaps there is something else that we need to discover to help us recover our balance and move forwards. That something is forgiveness, another secret of the afterlife.

4 | Secrets of Forgiveness

FORGIVENESS is perhaps the most important single process that brings peace to our soul and harmony to our life. All of us have been hurt at some point and wounded by the actions or words of another person. Sometimes the grievances have been so great we may have thought, 'No way, I'm not going to forgive them for this!' For various reasons, tension, arguments and conflict with those who are closest to us, especially blood relatives, can be worse than with anyone else. Resentment and hostility can run so deep that forgiveness becomes very difficult. Yet at the same time, if we can't resolve that which divides us in our families, I wonder how we think we have a chance of solving the bigger problems in the world. We may never forget but we can still choose to forgive.

The fact is that we are in charge of what we think, what we are and what we become. The only person standing in your way is you. Nobody will ever criticise and hate you as much as you are capable of hating yourself. And nobody will love you as much as you can love yourself. When you look back at your life – as you inevitably will at some point

– will you be pleased with what you see? Probably not. You will wish that you had spent more time with the people you truly loved, that you had figured out what mattered earlier on and that you hadn't wasted time on inconsequential things.

Learning to forgive a person or life situation invariably requires that we include ourselves as part of what needs forgiveness. We often think of forgiveness as something that someone who has done us wrong must ask of *us*. There is always another way of looking at something. My thoughts on forgiveness suggest that you focus on offering forgiveness to the person who has wronged you. Forgiveness is a gift we give to ourselves. It is not something we do for someone else. It isn't complicated. It's simple. Just identify the situation to be forgiven and ask yourself: 'Am I willing to waste my energy further on this matter?' If the answer is 'No,' then that's it! All is forgiven. It's not that big a deal if you don't make it out to be.

Forgiveness is an act of the imagination. It dares us to imagine a better future, one that is based on the possibility that our hurt will not be the final word on the matter.

'The weak can never forgive. Forgiveness is the attribute of the strong.'

Mahatma Gandhi

Forgiveness challenges us to give up our destructive thoughts about a situation and to believe in the possibility of a better future. It builds confidence that we can survive the pain and grow from it. Telling someone is a bonus! It is not necessary for forgiveness to begin the process that heals the hurt. Forgiveness often has little or nothing to do with another person because forgiveness is an internal matter. Forgiveness is about our own attitude and the grudges that we decide to hold on to.

A Lady with Great Expectations

We were in a private sitting. The lady in front of me was not, let's say, the friendliest person I've ever met. Her pinched face wore a dogged expression: an expression that seemed to say 'OK, I'm here but you'd better give me something I want!' I meet many people like her; people who have this almost permanent air of hostility around them. She said she was here because she wanted to connect with her mother.

'Audrey – that's your mother's name,' I began.

The lady nodded. It was rather a stern nod and you could see the tightness in her facial expression. She wasn't going to give an inch.

'Your mother's here with me,' I continued. 'She wants me to pass on her heartfelt thanks to you for trying to look after her at the end.'

'Hmm. Well, I had no choice really,' the lady scowled.

I pressed on: 'Audrey is telling me that she is grateful for the work you put in to find the nursing home. She realises it wasn't easy and not the most pleasant of tasks.'

Now, I don't know about you, but I think that's a lovely message to receive from someone who has passed over. It's just the sort of message that many people wish they would receive. But sometimes it's not enough and in this case it clearly wasn't – the lady wasn't moved in the slightest. She just muttered something under her breath.

I continued with the communication. 'She says she doesn't want you to feel guilty for that, as it was the best thing.'

'Yes, well it wasn't the best thing for me, was it?' the lady snapped.

I don't like to show my feelings in front of people about their reactions to the messages I give them because it's not my place to pass judgement. Besides which, I'm only being given access to a small part of their lives so I have to keep my distance and not respond. I calmly explained, 'She understands it has eaten into your inheritance but she says you still have enough to buy a house.'

The woman snorted and folded her arms. 'Well, what would she know? She wasn't much use to me in life and now she's not in death really!'

As you can imagine I was taken aback by her attitude. It was hard not to be – this woman had harboured enormous expectations of what her mother was supposed to do for her. I also felt that since her mother had made the effort to come through to her it would have been nice if she could be a bit gracious towards her. But what could I do? At times like this – and fortunately there have been few – I question the motivations of people who want to communicate with those who have passed over. I felt that this woman's expectations of her mother, Audrey, were simply not reasonable. They had nothing to do with her mother's needs and everything to do with her. And that wasn't really very fair.

Secret: loved ones in the afterlife often show a generosity and warmth that we would do well to imitate.

If we truly love and care about the happiness of the people in our lives – whether they be family or friends – we cannot burden them with our unrealistic expectations, even in the afterlife, or bind them to selfish and blind promises. Yet there are many examples of this. The woman who vows never to allow her parents to be put into a residential home may be showing a deep devotion to them, but circumstances may prevail to make that impossible. Similarly, the parent facing old age who binds his child to such a pledge is using emotional blackmail. This is bound to result in little else but pain and guilt. In an ideal world we would all hope to honour commitments made out of love but we have to be honest enough to know when it's just not possible. And sometimes events conspire in such a way that things are not clear cut, and we have to make the best decision we can for the greater good, even if that decision might not always suit us.

Danielle's Responsibility

A medium has to be fast on his feet. When the messages come to you they arrive in fragments, often very quick ones rather like a film being speeded up. It's my job to be able to put those fragments together. And those bits and pieces can be anything from a sense of a spirit's presence to noises and vivid pictures. When you're on the stage under hot lights, you really have to concentrate to make sense of it all, believe me.

I was on tour and on this occasion I felt I was being impressed upon by a gentleman who was directing me over to the right side of the room. 'I'm up in that row some-where,' I explained. 'And I'm wondering who's wearing a jacket of a loved one who has passed over.'

'I've got my grandad's cardigan,' piped up one woman.

'I've got my dad's fishing jacket at home,' said another.

'Goodness darlings, this is starting to sound like an auction!' I exclaimed. The audience laughed, which immediately made everybody more relaxed.

I focused my thoughts. 'Now the second lady there, I'm sure it's you. What's your name, my love?'

'Danielle,' she replied, straightening up in her seat.

'Danielle, I have the feeling that you wore this jacket to go out in the garden.'

She smiled. 'I suppose it might sound silly but I've used it to go out in. I've worn it in all sorts of places, even over evening dresses.'

'Well, that certainly does show a sense of individual

style!' There were more laughs from the audience. I waited for calm, then said, 'My love, something happened between the fourteenth and fifteenth of June 1987. Something that concerns a pale blue Metro.'

'Yes, that would be correct.'

'He's making a very clear reference to June 1987.'

Her eyes lit up. 'I know what it is now. My dad always went fishing on the fourteenth and fifteenth of June. He started doing it seventeen years ago with my husband and they never ever missed a date.'

'OK.' I focused carefully and then explained, 'I'm really very sorry for this guy because it's like he's really determined to get through, but he doesn't like doing this.' I directly looked at the woman, who was staring intently at me. 'My love, when Dad passed from this side of life, there was a horrible smell, wasn't there? He made the comment that he couldn't stand the smell of the place he was in. It was something to do with his illness.'

'Yes,' she agreed. She added: 'He hated the hospital. The minute he walked in he just wanted to turn and run.'

'I don't blame him, Danielle. We all hate that smell,' I confided. 'But back to him. He was so vocal about hating it at the time, that now he's telling me he's feeling a bit bad he made such a big fuss about being in hospital.'

Danielle laughed. 'Well, I hope he's listening properly, because he needn't feel guilty at all!'

I smiled back at her. 'My love, you made a reference earlier to something about fishing. Your dad is trying to show me that he is either happy about a younger man having had his stuff passed on to him, or he wants his stuff passed on to a younger lad.'

'Yes, I understand that.'

'Just tell him to be careful of the knife.'

'Right, I understand that,' Danielle nodded.

'Because the last fishing trip he went on he had had that knife sharpened and it's very sharp. Now Danielle, I have a message for your mum.'

'A message for Mum? What is it?' she asked hesitantly.

'I'm sorry, Mum will have to listen to this, but when eventually it's Mum's time to go and join him, he trusts you to make sure there'll be no arguments.'

'Thanks, Dad.' She paused and then looked at me questioningly, 'Why is he worrying about that, I wonder?'

'Well,' I explained, 'he's actually a bit irritated there was such a fuss when he passed over.'

'Oh, no!' Danielle looked shocked.

'It's all right, he's just saying, 'I don't want to see that sort of arguing that happened when I passed over when your mum eventually comes over and joins me."

'It won't,' Danielle said firmly.

'Now he wants to thank you. He wants to show his gratitude to you especially, Danielle, for making sure his song was played. He's saying, "It was very upsetting for everybody, but thank you for insisting that was what I wanted."'

At this point Danielle became quite emotional for the first time. There were the beginnings of tears in her eyes but she was still smiling as she said: 'Oh, Dad – thank *you*.'

'All right sir, OK,' I replied to Danielle's father, as I continued to relay his message. 'And the last little thing he is putting through is, will you make sure you're the one who goes to the furniture shop with Mum? Because if you don't they will get it all wrong. Do you understand what he's talking about?'

'I understand fully what he's talking about,' Danielle affirmed.

'Ever the practical man, that's what I feel about him.'

'Absolutely.' Danielle nodded in agreement, and then looked straight at me as she asked, 'But why me, Dad?'

'He's just responded to what you've said: because you listen to what your mum wants and you don't tell her what to do. You have the power in your hands to make things happen. He trusts you. Your dad loves you very much.'

'Yes, I love him too. My dad was a wonderful man; he was the best Dad ever, I loved my dad to bits.' Danielle wiped a tear from the corner of her eye. 'He wasn't strict, but he was firm and fair. If you mucked about he would tell you what he thought. Not in a heavy way though.'

'He's feeling a bit bad that he made them feel guilty about him being in hospital,' I continued.

She explained, 'He actually passed with cancer. In the end he was taken into hospital where he died. He always thought that people there were fussing around him; it wasn't that he didn't want the care; he just didn't want the fuss. He always thought he would be OK; he wasn't a man to go to the doctors for a little pain.'

'Clearly he's a little bit irritated that there was such a ridiculous fuss when he passed over,' I affirmed.

'When my dad passed, there was a family split, a big family rift. And it's still the same, so I suspect that's why he's talking about Mum. He just wants us all to get our act together and I assure you, Colin, I will do my best to make sure we give him that. But it's hard…' Danielle's voice trailed away.

I wanted to offer her some comfort: 'It seems he trusts you to make sure there will be no arguments.'

'The trouble is I can imagine when my mum passes it will split my family even more, so in that sense I understand what my dad is talking about; that he doesn't want any more divisions in the family. But, you know, that's big families for you. Ours is a large family and everybody in it wants different things,' Danielle explained. But then she concluded: 'We're going to have to do our very best to listen and maybe stop thinking about ourselves for a bit.' She had clearly taken her dad's message to heart.

Secret: we all have the power to make change happen and our loved ones are willing to encourage and support us from the afterlife.

Sometimes difficult relationships need someone who, even though the situation's not their fault, will come forward and say, 'Right, I'm going to do something here.' There always has to be a first move and a compromise but it has to be sincere and not done for purely personal gain. Swallowing our pride is a big mouthful sometimes but the alternative does not taste so good either.

However, for many people the idea of forgiving someone is a major step. They might feel that it's not in them naturally to forgive, that perhaps it's not part of their personal philosophy or that it may show weakness if they do so. Meeting so many people who are looking for some sort of redress from someone they have lost has been personally very eye-opening and helped me learn a lot about myself.

A Family Unresolved

There seemed to be a lot of people crammed into the studio on this particular day. I had no idea why but we seemed to have an even larger crowd than usual. The people who look after such things finally got them all organised and we were ready to begin.

The images were zooming into my head: 'I've got to be up here in the third row. I'm absolutely sure of that and I've got this gentleman with me who I feel that he's trying to connect with his son or grandson. And the first word that he's putting or trying to put in my mind is like "breakdown".'

I noticed a man in his forties. Although there was nothing about him physically that made him stand out, I just had an overwhelming sense that he was the intended recipient of this communication.

I spoke to him: 'Sir, I'd like to ask you your name, because every time I look along this line, my eye keeps falling on you for some reason. I've got this gentleman here who feels like Grandad trying to connect, and he's saying something about somebody having a breakdown. What sort of breakdown I don't exactly know. But it leads me to think they're talking about you.'

Jim was the man's name and he replied that it was very likely him the communication was for, although he didn't sound sure. That's not surprising: many of the audience think it will be someone else who's picked out so they tend to be taken unaware of a message's relevance for them, even if the information is strong.

'All right, Jim,' I continued. 'I feel that this man is talking about you.'

'That's interesting.' Jim thought for a moment. 'I mean, I don't talk to my father any more. Maybe the breakdown side is there, but I don't know for sure.'

'Jim, your grandfather is now impressing on me a very emotional feeling and the way that my mind receives this connection is that it seems to be about a lost opportunity. Does your father see his grandchildren?'

'I don't think so,' said Jim.

'What a lost opportunity. I'm getting the name Celia.'

'That's my sister!' Jim exclaimed, adding, 'That's freaked me out.'

I told him that the spirits like to use these bits of information to identify themselves.

'So, what about these lost opportunities?' I said, returning to the point.

'Obviously my dad is losing out on certain things as we grow up, specifically the grandchildren. There have been certain communication breakdowns within the family, so I can only think the lost opportunities are about that. It makes perfect sense now.'

I said, 'He's asking you to sit and talk about this. Your grandfather is appealing to you to talk about the situation relating to Dad.' I observed, 'Dad's got a hearing problem; he doesn't hear so well any more.'

'He's always had a problem hearing, but the difference is he's not hard of hearing,' said Jim.

'But he has problems hearing,' I emphasised. 'Do you understand what he's saying, Jim? – He's telling me Dad does not listen. There are things that need to be said, things that have been fermenting – shall we say – for many years, longer than you've been around. He says, "There's been enough fighting in my family and it's time for it to end!"'

'Yes, I understand that.'

'And he's appealing to you to make a start; enough is enough.' I paused, then asked, 'Who is Joe?'

'That would be my dad.'

'OK Jim, Grandad really does send his love, but you've got to deliver the message.'

'It would be down to me, wouldn't it!' Jim snorted.

He later explained to me, 'When I was told I had to deliver the message I really felt reluctant. In a way, I wish my grandad hadn't put this responsibility on my shoulders, because life is hard enough as it is, but I guess if anyone has got to make the first move it will have to be me, to put things right between people. The onus usually is on me anyway, it seems. So I'm sure I'll be making a few social visits when I get back home. This experience has definitely been an eye-opener; it does make it harder to disbelieve when you come out with all those little details, so yes, I can honestly say it has probably converted me.'

He shrugged his shoulders, but seemed willing enough to accept the task his grandad had given him.

Secret: our loved ones are constantly watching over us, wanting us to avoid conflict and make resolutions where possible.

It is truly impossible to start afresh and to make clear, healthy, life-giving choices until we have let go of past hurts, confusion and resentments. Old wounds have a drawing power and pull our attention to them over and over, taking energy and hope from us, preventing us from starting again. Forgiveness is a creative act that changes us from prisoners of the past to liberated people at peace with our memories. It is not forgetfulness, but it involves accepting the promise that the future can be more than dwelling on memories of past injury. There is no future in the past.

True wealth

Stories like this one, typical of the Sufi tradition, have been told through time to pass on wisdom:

A wise woman who was travelling in the mountains found a precious stone in a stream.

The next day she met another traveller who was hungry, and the wise woman opened her bag to share her food. The hungry traveller saw the precious stone and asked the woman to give it to him.

She did so without hesitation.

The traveller left rejoicing in his good fortune. He knew the stone was worth enough to give him security for a lifetime. But, a few days later, he came back to return the stone to the wise woman.

'I've been thinking,' he said. 'I know how valuable this stone is, but I give it back in the hope that you can give me something even more precious. Give me what you have within you that enabled you to give me this stone.'

Sometimes it's not the wealth you have but what's inside you that others need.

The First to Forgive

I always feel honoured to witness the joy and enlighten-
ment of communications from those who are in spirit.
Spirits work in mysterious ways and are involved in our
day-to-day lives in ways we do not know. They also watch
out for us and help to keep us on the right track.

It was a bit chilly that day, but the theatre was full and
the mood was expectant. The lights came on as we started
the show. I found that I was seeing a handful of chits. By
that, I mean tickets like you see at the horse races – betting
tickets.

I began, 'Hello, I'm getting the sense of a gentleman
here and he's showing me something like Ladbrokes or
William Hill – you know, the bookies.

'He spent a lot of time in there if it's who I think it is,' a
voice piped up from the audience. There were a few smiles.

I turned to the speaker. 'Hello, my love. What's your
name?'

'Gail.'

'Gail, your father is showing me a little one who has
gone over into the spirit. He's telling me he always had a
great love for children and that for him the saddest thing
was knowing the little one had passed over. Your dad is a
man of kind heart and deeds.'

Gail agreed, 'Yes he is, Colin. The child he's talking
about was my sister's.' She was silent for a moment,
obviously feeling very emotional.

'He didn't really live that long, did he?' I said.

'No, he wasn't on this earth for long. He died of cot death at the age of five months,' she replied in a choked voice.

'I can see blonde curly hair. Lots of lovely curly locks.'

'Yes, Colin. Although he didn't have much hair when he died it would almost have certainly turned out to be fair and curly,' she said and went on, 'I looked after him when he was born. In fact I took over from my sister who … well, she had a lot of problems in her life, physically and emotionally. I don't want to go into those now but I think I was closer to the baby. And…' At this point she broke down and began to cry. The woman next to her placed a comforting hand on hers.

It's hard sometimes to know when to continue with a communication. You can only trust your intuition, but after a moment or two she looked able to carry on. 'I think I would have been closer to him,' she said, wiping her eyes. 'I think I would have had him in the end.'

'It sounds to me, my love, that you and your sister have got something to sort out between you.'

'Just being in the same room as her at the moment gets on my nerves. It drives me crazy and I can't say what it is,' she confessed.

At that point I felt that it might be worth taking the heat off her for a bit and just talking about the forgiveness that so needed to happen here. So I said, 'I just want to make the point that I know how hard it is to forgive. When you feel that forgiveness is necessary, remember you're not just doing it for the sake of the other person. You're doing it for yourself. It would be great if other people would come to you and ask forgiveness but you must accept the fact that some will never do that. But that's their choice. They do not need to be forgiven, or at least that's what they think. They did what they did and that is it – except for the consequences, which they must live with. And frankly that is hard enough for them.'

Gail spoke up: 'I know what it is that needs to be said. But I can't really say it now in front of everyone here. But when I get home, yes, I will phone her.'

'I have the feeling that you really do need to sort it out once and for all. You know, if this little boy had survived you would have adored him. And that's the message the little boy's been brought forward today to say: whatever's between you and your sister, sort it out. Can you under-stand that?'

'Absolutely. Yes, I do.'

'And it's your dad who's made it all possible because he loves kids. He was a good man. You really do need to sort it out once and for all,' I repeated.

'Dad was and is a very kind-hearted man. Wouldn't say boo to a goose. He passed over thirty-five years ago,' Gail told me.

Later, at the end of the show Gail came up to talk to me. I sensed she was ready to make a transition but was finding it hard. I spent a few minutes talking to her and pointed out that the hurts wouldn't begin to heal until there was forgiveness, but that it sounded that she would be the one ready to offer it. Recovery from wrongdoing that produces genuine forgiveness takes time. For some, it may take years. I told her that it was important she didn't rush it and that constantly opening up old hurts would be unhelpful.

 **Secret:** it may fall to us to be the one who forgives first but we should not shrink from that responsibility for it has obviously been given to us for a reason.

Happily, it seems that once we have passed over we are usually able to rejoice in the good times we have shared rather than dwell on what went wrong. It also seems that many of the negative aspects of relationships get left behind when we pass over. Expressions such as 'I will never forgive that person for betraying me'; 'if I never see them again it will be too soon'; 'I will never forgive them for lying to me/cheating on me/treating me badly' all become unimportant in the afterlife. But this doesn't mean that we all skip lightly off over the rainbow to a land of everlasting happiness! However, it does mean we are able to see the value even in brief encounters we have given and received. And for those where an enduring bond – soul to soul and spirit to spirit – has been forged, the journey we share in the afterlife is most likely an eternal one.

The truth is that often there are no easy answers to any

situation, although that can be hard to accept. People often think mediums can explain why something happened and there have been times when I wish I could! One thing I do know about the spirit world is that the way in which a person dies does not doom them to be some sort of outcast when they pass over. They will still be the person that we knew and loved.

The Girl Who Became Whole

When I first met Kerry and Alison, the two girls had different expectations. Kerry had been convinced that her friend Alison would get her mum coming through, but she was absolutely sure that nobody in the spirit world would come through for herself, which was fine with me. In a way I prefer it that way: when there is a connection people are pleasantly surprised, which is better than holding high expectations and then not having the spirit come through, as can happen.

When I pointed at Kerry and asked her whether she had a father in spirit she suddenly sat up and paid attention. It turned out that the man in question was her real father but she hadn't grown up with him.

As I relayed the message, Kerry was speechless at first; then she explained: 'I last saw my real father when I was about four years old. It was very emotional because everyone was telling him to go away, to get out of our lives and to never, ever come back again. As you can imagine, at the age of four I was old enough to remember things but I didn't really understand what was going on. Dad said he loved me and then he left.'

'That was the last time you saw him.'

'Yes, it was.'

'He's telling me that those people called him the devil and made it sound like he was some kind of gangster or something, which he certainly wasn't. He was a good man, my darling.'

Kerry turned pale. 'I was always brought up with the idea that my dad must be one of the worst, nastiest, most unkind people around. That was the impression I've got from family and friends.'

'You weren't even allowed to say his name.'

'Yes, and if I was naughty as a child, there would be the inevitable comment, "Oh, you're so like your father." So I've always walked around thinking that there must be this bad part of me that shouldn't ever be allowed to come to the surface.'

'But you loved him all the same?' I ventured.

'Yes, though it feels like a big secret, almost like a fantasy.'

'Well, I can tell you that that side of you is just fine and Dad was not as bad as he's been made out to be. He sent you a letter, didn't he?'

Kerry's eyes widened. She looked elated but stunned. She said, 'Yes, but they didn't let me read it. I didn't hear anything from him until I was about twelve and then he sent this beautiful diamante necklace and earrings. I remember my mother saying, "Fancy sending a twelve-year-old a present like that!" She took the letter away from me, as well as the necklace and earrings, and I never saw them again. But I read enough of the letter to know I was loved.'

A year later, I met Kerry and Alison again and I was impressed to discover that Kerry had found a new purpose in her life. She had mastered the art of Reiki, the Japanese spiritual healing discipline, which has its roots in ancient Shinto teachings. 'What made you do it?' I wondered.

'Well, someone suggested it to me and I'd been procrastinating about it. You know I'd always wanted to do something in the "helping" area of work to make people feel better. And after that reading last year, I felt like a whole person, a better person, and I thought, "You can do this, you're worthy and you're not all that bad stuff." It was like a huge weight had been lifted from my shoulders and it was just amazing. Since then I've felt the future is like an endless road of possibilities, rather than before when it was very cloudy. Now I've got this amazing feeling of freedom: that I can do whatever I want to do and I really feel that's down to being able to have this contact with my dad.'

'She really has come a long way, Colin,' agreed Allison. 'It's amazing how she's just more open as a person. I just think this connection with her father, however brief, has allowed her to believe in herself and it has validated her place in the world.'

I knew Kerry had been through bereavements in her family in the last year and asked her how she had coped.

'My mother and stepfather have both died but I have coped very well and I think that's because I know they are around,' she said honestly. 'I feel that I'm a new person and I don't care what anybody thinks of me.'

 Secret: there is always the possibility for a new start in life no matter what has gone before.

The greatest misconception about forgiveness is the belief that forgiving the incident, such as an affair for example, means that you condone it and think it's OK. That's not exactly true. Forgiveness does not mean that you have to reconcile with someone who treated you badly. Another misconception is that it depends on whether the person who did you wrong apologises, wants you back, or changes his or her ways. If another person's poor behaviour were the primary determinant for your healing then the unkind and selfish people in your life would retain power over you indefinitely. Forgiveness is the experience of finding peace inside and can be neither compelled nor stopped by another. I believe that to withhold forgiveness is to choose to continue to remain the victim. Remember, you always have a choice.

Stella and Roger

It was an October morning some time ago when Stella arrived at my house for a private sitting. I noted from my diary that the appointment had been made months before, on 19 May – my birthday, so I felt that maybe this was an omen for a good sitting.

As we settled ourselves down with a cup of tea I began to explain to Stella what she could reasonably expect from a sitting and what may or may not happen. It is my way to explain to every sitter that in effect what we are doing is an experiment and even if nothing happens, they really shouldn't take this as being ominous: it just means the time is not right.

One of the criticisms often levelled at mediums by sceptics is that we read the body language of sitters. Well, yes we do; in fact, I think it's important for a medium to observe the sitter. Why? Well, in that way we can judge how to present the communication we are sensing from the spirit communicator. Although a medium should never change the facts of the communicated evidence, it is important that what you present – although it may be difficult and/or negative – is not delivered like a blow from an axe to an already fragile person.

Stella was an attractive lady in her mid-fifties who seemed to be making a great effort to hold her emotions in check and to give an outward appearance to the world of self-reliant composure. However, as I discovered, the truth was a different matter.

I felt the communication come through very clearly. 'I have a gentleman here by the name of Roger. He tells me that you carry his wedding ring and would love to wear it, but you feel it's inappropriate.' I passed this first piece of evidence to Stella.

Her reaction was a curious one: she began to laugh and cry at the same time. 'Only I ever called him Roger, and that was after the cartoon character Roger the Dodger. It was my pet name for him and he was my husband.' She dabbed her eyes with a tissue and settled back into the chair.

'But you were not his wife at the time of his death,' I said. 'He shows me that by this time, although you remained close, you had divorced.'

Stella confirmed this to be correct. As the details of the communication started to unfold it became apparent that a great deal of affection existed between Stella and Roger, but he had indeed been a rogue. He was always involved in dodgy business deals, some of which were not quite legal. On a personal note he had loads of affairs which she had turned a blind eye to for many years.

Ultimately Roger was arrested, charged and imprisoned for three years for one of his illegal business scams. The full extent of his wrongdoings soon became common knowledge and he and Stella divorced.

Once the anger had subsided, the pair became good friends following the divorce and would often meet up for dinner. They once even spent a holiday together with their grown-up children in the South of France.

Much to everyone's surprise, Roger then married a woman much younger than him. His children strongly disapproved and many arguments ensued. What was interesting was that when the situation got bad he turned to Stella for help and she very kindly stepped in, calming things with the children on his behalf. She did this even though she herself was hurting badly, and went so far as to be on friendly terms with the wife.

In the summer of 1990, Roger had a massive and very unexpected heart attack. He died instantly. The funeral was a very painful occasion for Stella, watching all their friends and family offering their condolences to Roger's new wife. Few people seemed to know what to say to Stella herself. So there she stood, on the outer perimeters of the funeral party, desperately looking for an appropriate time and space to escape from this situation.

As she said to me when she first sat down, 'I'm the grieving widow but with no husband to grieve over; he was taken from me before he was dead and I'm fed up with being so bloody adult about it. I'm angry and can't forgive him for leaving me in this situation.'

Then Roger began to express his feelings to me to pass on to Stella. I explained, 'He regrets that he caused the break-up of your marriage: he feels it was all his fault.'

The tears welled up in Stella's eyes again.

'Even though he remarried he still loves you; he never stopped loving you. He's pleased that you have the wedding ring with you.'

I'm happy to say that at this point Stella's tears began to subside and in fact she was smiling as she talked about him. 'Even when he was an inconsiderate bastard, he made me laugh,' she confided.

And so we talked and she decided she would not focus on the bad things, but instead on the fact that they had fun together and produced three wonderful children. I suggested that all relationships change and if we focus on the parts of them we left behind, it stops us enjoying what they become. We have to accept what they become, whether we like it or not.

I never met Stella again but recently found a letter she sent to me a few months after our sitting. In it she told me how much happier and clearer she felt about things after the sitting and that she now realised Roger the Dodger had loved her despite all the heartache. She was going to enjoy those memories.

I recently heard that Stella had passed over. I'm sure she must have met up with Roger and I hope for both of them he is better behaved on that side of life!

Secret: allowing ourselves to be trapped by feelings such as anger and regret prevents us from being able to enjoy the many things we have shared with our loved ones.

I would say that many of the communications that take place between those on the spirit side and those who are in the physical world consist of things unsaid and also of regrets for what was left unsaid when they passed over. In these instances, I feel especially privileged that I am able to pass on messages that can help to heal old wounds and move relationships on to fresh understandings.

Saying It When It Matters

I remember the time I met Danny; the two of us were discussing plans for a new show. We were taking our time, calmly going over the details. The office windows looked out over a cityscape of roof tops and balconies. Then, as I sat talking to Danny, his father came through to me.

'Danny,' I said, 'someone here is very interested in using their hands ... I see boxing gloves.'

Danny put his pile of papers to one side and looked curiously at me. 'My father enjoyed physical sports. He wanted me to box.'

'I'm getting the impression that he tried to make you do those things when you weren't very interested in them.'

Danny appeared shocked. His face flushed. 'Ah, yes. But he wasn't always like that,' he said quickly. 'It just seemed to get really intense as we got older.'

'He's coming through and telling me that he wants you to know that he's fully aware there were some difficult times with him.'

Danny smiled wryly. 'Times? More like difficult years!'

I listened carefully and passed the message on: 'Danny, he tells me he regrets those times, but he wants to say that just because he pushed you it didn't and doesn't mean there was no love there. In fact, he's saying that he reckons you two were actually very close.'

'Hmm.' Danny didn't look particularly convinced. 'I guess he's just trying to say that's the way he is,' he said. 'That would be Dad's way.'

But there was more to it than that: 'He's sorry, Danny. Sorry for not being everything he should have been to you and for not paying more attention to what you might have wanted from him. He wishes he hadn't tried to make you something you didn't want to be.'

Danny rubbed his chin in thought, then said: 'I'm sorry too. I wish I'd said the things I wanted to say to him. I guess we both stood back and waited for the other – and of course if you do that nothing happens.'

I carried on with the message: 'Danny, he's saying that he does love you and he wants you to know he approves of you. Do you understand that?'

'Yes.' Danny looked straight at me.

'He wants you to have his support and love.'

'Thank you. But I think I've learned we should say things and we should tell people we love them. I'm glad Dad has come through now, though.'

After a moment's reflective silence, we both carried on with the paperwork in front of us.

Secret: we can let people know we love them, even when they have passed over. But it also reminds us of the need to say something while they are still with us.

Another part of my work I find particularly rewarding is when a communication helps somebody to look at a relationship in a completely new light in such a way that it helps them in their life in the here and now. This might mean revisiting the past and it can also mean finding a new way forward into the future.

The Boy Who Was Left behind

You know how you look at some people and you think, 'Gosh they're tough.' I recall meeting such a bloke a couple of years ago. The communication told me that he was one of four boys involved in a childhood accident of some sort. He came forward from the audience as soon as I mentioned it and there were tears in his eyes. It appeared that when they were children, he, his brother and two mates were making a dugout: they'd been at it an awfully long time and had dug quite a lot so there was a lot of dirt and debris. In the event, it fell in on them, burying the others but allowing him to wriggle free. The others were killed.

After it happened his parents became distant from him. It was as if they couldn't love him because his brother was not there. They were simply unable to move on. His life was almost paralysed in some ways.

Now, his brother came through to me. I looked at the sorrowful figure in front of me, and assured him: 'He's telling me he's not angry with you.' You could see the man's eyes brighten up, tearful as he was. I continued: 'He doesn't blame you for what happened and he doesn't want you to feel guilty.'

I see a lot of relieved people in my audiences; however, you could just feel this man's relief at this brief but important message. He came to me afterwards and said, 'Thank you, Colin. You have just set me free. I have a marriage and children and now I know it's OK. I know that my brother doesn't blame me and still loves me. I can now continue my life in peace.'

Secret: we all need to be set free. The afterlife teaches us that if we are able to give someone the peace they seek, then we should do so.

Blame is a funny thing. It can keep us trapped in the past and it can also mean that we find fault with everyone except ourselves, looking outwards but rarely inwards. I find it very odd sometimes that those in authority seem to be happy to stand up and talk about how society could be better, yet they don't work on their own relationships. I suppose my role means I get to see a great deal of hypocrisy inherent in most people's lives. Now I'm certainly not perfect, but I know my faults and I try to work on them! It would be good for those of us who yearn for a happier, more harmonious community to look first at our own relationships and to work on these. The inescapable fact is that what we do inside our family units, with friends and work colleagues has an effect on the wider world. When you think about it, it's common sense.

When I was at school (and I'm sure when you were too) I got into a few scrapes but being a very convincing talker I was able to duck and dive and eventually worm my way out of it *and* find someone else to take the blame. You know the sort of thing: 'He started it. I didn't!' There is, I think, an inherent desire on the part of human beings to decide what is 'wrong' and what is 'right'. And I know in the past that if I thought I had been 'wronged' then I would expect someone else to ask for my forgiveness. But as I've got older I've realised that you can't expect rational explanations when life throws up random events. Sometimes you have to learn to say 'it is what it is,' deal with it as graciously as you can and move on. I'm still learning.

The Woman Who Wanted Someone to Blame

I was appearing at a lovely old theatre on the coast a few years ago. We'd been staying not far away at a charming seaside hotel so, rather than take the car, I decided to walk to the theatre in the early evening. It was a lovely night, not warm but clear and very still. As I walked by the railings, I could hear the sound of the sea as the waves lapped below. It was one of those moments when you think, 'Well, just enjoying this is actually what life's all about.'

Soon it was time for the show to start.

I think maybe it was the third or fourth communication that came through. I sensed a young man coming through and I also had the impression a violent death was involved. I asked, 'Does anyone here know a boy who was murdered at a young age?'

There were several shocked gasps, but of course it had to be the woman who I'd noticed in the front row. She stepped forward.

'Hello, my love,' I greeted her and then began: 'The boy who was murdered was your son.'

'Yes, he was,' she said. 'And he was innocent,' she added firmly.

I learned that her son had been murdered by two travellers he'd become involved with. This boy – we'll call him Al – got involved with two lads who were travellers. They were selling ecstasy pills in the Essex area when one night there was argument and the boy was stabbed. One of the boys was convicted of the murder but the other one got off because the police were unable to prove he was there. But the mother of the dead boy was utterly convinced that both of them had been involved.

It had been three years since it happened and this poor woman could find no peace. The problem appeared to be that she did not agree with the court's decision not to convict the second traveller.

She was just so angry. 'I warned my son about those people but he never listened!' she exploded. Her anger seemed so fierce I wondered what any communication could do for her at this point.

She said, 'Since it happened the family has been in disarray and we haven't been able to get any peace.'

'Al is telling me that he was responsible,' I explained quietly.

'No,' she said, 'he can't be. It was them. They made him do it.'

'He's saying to me to tell you that it was his choice to be there and that while he knew he wasn't a bad person, he had done a bad thing and paid the ultimate penalty.'

'But they took him from me,' she said bitterly. 'Why didn't they die?'

I could feel her pain and anger. Tears welled up in her eyes and then she started nodding. There was a long pause and everyone in the audience went quiet.

I broke the silence. 'My love, he wants you to move on. Accept his part in this and move on. It's all right.' Al wanted his mother to acknowledge that, while he wasn't responsible for the fact his life was taken, he was responsible for his own actions and involvement. She had to forgive him, them and herself.

Forgiving doesn't necessarily mean interacting with those who have wronged you but it must be something you do to set yourself free. Have you noticed that if you keep picking at a scab it will never heal? Our loved ones who have passed over do not want us seeking revenge on their behalf. That sort of attitude is destructive to everyone: it destroys our good memories and stops us moving on. One of the key spiritual laws which is so simple yet so true is that you can change nothing in life except yourself.

Secret: after the death of a loved one,
sooner or later we have to move on.
Otherwise we will remain stuck in
the moment our loved one left us.
That can't work for us or them.

It really is never too late to say sorry. An apology from the heart will always make a difference. Forgiving someone else means agreeing within yourself to overlook the wrong they have committed against you and to move on with your life. It's the only way. It means cutting them some slack.

'What?' you say! 'Be nice to them after what they did to me? Never!' But refusing to forgive keeps you tied up, not them. Being willing to forgive can bring a sense of peace and well-being and means you will lose that feeling of anxiety that will otherwise always be there.

However, forgiveness is not something we have to do, but something we must allow to flow through us. When we step away from the rational side of our human nature and allow ourselves to forgive, we can at that point move on to something better without all that bitterness, all that sense of injustice. We become aware that we are free and we can project that love outward into our world.

A Father's Remorse

Being a medium, at times I pick up some odd images, I really do. It can be quite disconcerting sometimes, especially when I get images of illness or even of body parts. And that's what was happening on this day in the studio. I was seeing blood and what I felt sure were internal organs. At the same time there seemed to be a date attached to the image; I explained: 'I see a man who was taken into hospital in 1972 to have an operation where he was cut and opened up from the back.'

A small woman with very dark eyes and a glossy black bob immediately put her hand up. She was called Angela. 'That would be my father,' she said. 'My father was the one who had a kidney removed, and – yes – it was in 1972.'

'Angela, my love, would you understand about there being unresolved anger over what should be done with Dad?' Angela told me that there had been a great deal of arguments and hence bad feeling about it.

I explained, 'Angela, what I need to do now is strengthen the connection. I feel as though what I'm getting here are thoughts from Dad that are somehow being passed on for him because he can't make the connection himself. Do you understand that?'

'Yes,' Angela replied.

'So would you please step down and come and join me here on the sofa so we can try to make this connection more powerful.' She came up to join me, and settled herself down. The connection grew stronger: 'He's being very hard on himself, very self-critical indeed.' I addressed the spirit himself: 'Sir, I don't think you should be like this.'

I turned once more to Angela. 'My love, this is a man who's carrying a lot of regret and unhappiness as a result.

He feels remorse and shame for his actions and he's asked to come forward and say that he got it very wrong indeed.'

'I can understand that well,' said Angela, a look of understanding in her eyes.

'All right. Now, does it make sense that he disowned part of his family in his earthly life?'

'Very much so unfortunately.' There was a note of bitterness in Angela's voice.

'Darling, he'd like to acknowledge that this was a very wrong thing to do. Although you weren't the only family member, he realises that you had to carry the family can and take a lot of responsibility for a very long time. He's saying that he feels that no woman – particularly at the age when you should have been free – should have had to do that and he'd like to apologise very much indeed.'

Angela was becoming teary. She took a sip of water as the audience watched and waited. 'Hmm. Yes,' she said, her voice thick with emotion.

'My love,' I continued, 'he didn't know how to express love and affection in his earthly life. He could flatter with wit but he had no idea how to let down his guard and express his true, deepest feelings.'

Angela sniffed, wiped away a tear and said she knew this and it hurt her more than ever because she still knew that he was capable of love and emotion.

'Angela, darling, he wants, no – he *needs* – to make this apology to you for all that you've suffered. And he hopes that even though he is on the spirit side, you can begin anew.'

As we talked, I learned that Angela's father was a Londoner who went to Scotland during the war. His marriage was a wartime one and, as with many of those hurried, spur-of-the-moment marriages, it broke up.

Angela told me, 'He was a very handsome man who could flirt. He liked the ladies and they liked him. Not surprisingly, he was quite cocky and irresponsible and really should never have got married. I suppose you'd call him a Jack the lad.'

I said that it felt like he left a lot of unravelled threads behind him when he passed.

'Well, he remarried and had a second family,' replied Angela. 'I finally managed to trace them and now we're in regular contact and get on very well. He actually made several attempts to come back to our family but by that time I was fifteen and my mother had brought us up. He offered to move up north in the hope of resurrecting the relationship but she felt that there was too much water under the bridge.'

'And what do you feel about this, Angela. Now, today?'

'It makes me feel very emotional, deeply so,' she admitted. 'And a little uncomfortable if I'm to tell the truth. But I'm also very relieved because it has resolved a great deal for me and, in one reading, given me some peace. I feel that we can now put a lot of things to rest and move on with our lives. But just as importantly my father can feel peace as well.'

Secret: it is never too late to lay anger to rest and start again.

My work exposes me to so many insights that I might otherwise not have had. Because I'm in the middle of communications between this life and the spiritual world, I naturally cannot fail to learn from the experiences of others. People have often asked me if certain things affect me. Of course they do! Sometimes you will hear a story and realise that there is something very similar playing out in your life. This is always likely to happen when, for example, I'm in conflict with a friend; invariably I will be involved in passing on a message where conflict is involved. And so I will then end up thinking about my own situation.

Sometimes, of course, it can be very hard to forgive because that assumes a kind of responsibility. Forgiveness can mean that we make our peace with other people, on this earthly plain or in the afterlife; but it can also mean that we forgive ourselves. To be honest, we will never be able to let go of past hurts if we don't forgive ourselves first.

A Family in Turmoil

During my 2005 tour, I was appearing in a lovely old theatre in a town in the north of England. It had been a tiring tour but it had been very rewarding for me and, I think, for my audiences. Sometimes if the stage lights are shining in slightly the wrong place it can be quite disorientating and on this particular night I was feeling a little unsettled by them. Still – the show must go on!

The communication came through from a young man called Steve who was keen to speak to his family. Steve impressed on me that he had been accidentally stabbed and he had made contact so that he might heal the terrible pain his family had suffered since his death. He asked me to ensure that another brother – one who was not in the audience – must try to find forgiveness. He believed that this brother's failure to forgive was causing the rest of the family complete hurt and pain. He told me that even though he was now in the spirit world he had no regrets about the actions he had taken since if he had not done so, it would have been another family member who was spirit side, not him!

Shielding my eyes against the bright lights, I delivered that communication to the family – mum, two sisters and a brother – and between them they agreed they would pass it on to the brother who had not come that evening.

I stepped to the side, out of the glare, where I could see the family more clearly. Steve then went on to relay a number of personal and evidential messages to them, but what he seemed to want most – and it came through with such force and strength – was to ask the brother who had come to the demonstration to stay behind and speak to me privately afterwards. This young man had sobbed uncontrollably throughout the communication but he nevertheless agreed to come and see me afterwards. I have to tell you this type of thing doesn't often happen but I felt the message that came through from Steve was so urgent I had a responsibility to see this through to wherever it was going.

Around forty minutes later the last stragglers left the theatre and made their way to the foyer for autographs. Before I went to meet them I made my way across the now empty auditorium and found the lone figure of Steve's brother who was, understandably, nervously fidgeting as he sat hunched in the seat he'd occupied throughout the show.

As I sat down in the chair beside him I once felt again the force of his brother Steve coming through. I began to speak to this sad young man as Steve showed me the tragic circumstances of his death and also the devastation, bitterness and acrimony it had created.

I discovered that the young man's name was Gary. He was just twenty-three years old but had already served time in prison and had apparently just been recently released. Through the communication I learned that Steve was the eldest brother in the family. There were three lads in all and Steve was only fifteen when their father abandoned the family. Not surprisingly he rapidly found himself thrust into the role of part-time breadwinner and carer. He had to support his mum, which meant helping her keep control of his brothers and sisters and also having to work after school. That meant he'd had to cut short his plans to go to technical college at sixteen and instead start work full time in a local factory to help support his family.

Since Steve and his mother both had to work at full-time jobs, the task of looking after the children of the family after school fell to an elderly neighbour known affectionately as Aunty Nellie. Gary was one of those children who was virtually impossible to control: it seemed to make no difference what anybody said or did. He seemed to suffer from hyperactivity and was never far away from trouble. It wasn't long before Gary began experimenting with solvent abuse and soon fell in with a pretty bad crowd and was introduced to heroin. Like many drug addicts, Gary had to find ways to afford his growing habit and turned to stealing – from his own family.

As we sat in the darkened and increasingly chilly auditorium, Gary confirmed that this was all true. At seventeen he had been at his lowest ebb, having stolen from and hurt his family to the point where his mum could not stand it anymore. Worried about his influence on the other children, she asked him to leave the family home. Gary told me he moved into a friend's council flat, which made things worse since that meant two heroin addicts living together. This did not stop him stealing from the family home; in fact, one day Gary broke in and took the television, leaving his mum in tears.

It was at this point that Steve decided enough was enough and he had to do something to keep the family together. He had stormed off to where Gary was living and planned to give him a bloody good hiding! On the way he changed his mind and decided instead that he was going to persuade his brother to seek help for his deadly addiction before it was too late. Steve banged loudly on the door and Gary opened in what must've been a state of high agitation. His dealer was late and he was badly in need of a fix. The last thing he needed was his stupid older brother screaming outside since it would only frighten his dealer off!

'Steve is telling me he wanted you to listen to him that day. He just wanted to get you the help he thought you needed,' I told Gary, who could barely nod as he was sobbing so hard.

Finally the tears slowed, he wiped his eyes with the heel of his hand and started to speak. 'I know but I just wanted him to go away. Why didn't he just listen to me and just pi** off? It was for his own good. If he had just gone, none of this business would have happened.' He was sobbing heavily again now. I felt very sad for him as it was evident he was in a deeply painful place.

I said, 'He couldn't just go, Gary. He was your brother and he felt he had to save you ... Steve is showing me a knife. He says that you lashed out and stabbed him.'

'Yes...' Gary choked, 'but I honestly don't remember what happened; honest to God, I don't.'

The pictures I was getting in my head were a virtual kaleidoscope of images that seemed to relate to Steve trying to reason with Gary. The knife appeared as if from nowhere and then suddenly Steve was on the floor, pale and bloodied. When it happened the police arrived forty minutes later to find Gary still standing over Steve, staring blankly ahead of him.

Gary went to trial but various things including the rehabilitation he had undertaken while on remand were taken into account, thus resulting in a relatively short sentence. But of course lots of damage was done to the family. As it turned out his long-suffering mother and sisters were willing to forgive him, but the surviving brother could not find it in himself to forgive Gary for killing Steve.

Gary still felt haunted and admitted that he struggled daily with the temptation to return to heroin in order to block out his emotions.

The message was coming to an end: Steve impressed one last thought into my mind to pass on to Gary: 'Do something good with your life and I will back you all the way.'

While most of us will never commit a wrongdoing that is as severe in its impact as Gary's, we all do things that hurt or upset others. Sometimes it goes so far that it reaches a point where we are unable to forgive ourselves. However, if there is an indication that the person whom we have wronged wants to offer forgiveness then I personally think we need to take it. It would be an even greater sin to refuse that forgiveness and continue to hold ourselves in a state of guilt when we have been given that opportunity to move on.

Secret: there is always time to forgive and be forgiven.

When I was young many of the older generation (thankfully not my own parents) held that crying was not a good thing to do. I often heard it said that if you cried too much, 'you're going to make yourself sick.' Crying, especially in public, was definitely bad news. In short, crying, even when grieving, was considered to be a sign of weakness. Through the years this and many other natural ways of showing emotion have been stifled by, for example, celebrities who assume a stoic pose when appearing on camera. (I can remember the death of President Kennedy and the way Jackie showed little emotion during the funeral and on TV.)

Expressing emotion in general – such as happiness, anger, love or sadness – was frowned upon for years in western culture. Add to this the fact that quite often in families there is this tacit, unwritten agreement that since you are part of the same family, you care for each other and that is that – there's no need to actually show you care. And for some people that means they need not do very much more. But love isn't just a word, a thought or about sharing the same surname as someone else: it's about actions and learning to do kind and compassionate things for others.

The Doors are Always Open

Sometimes those who have passed over make contact because they have unresolved issues and are looking to their loved ones in the physical world for acknowledgement of something that is troubling them. The following story is typical of this sort of communication.

We'd added an extra show in Birmingham to the tour and the tickets had sold out very quickly, which I was pleased about. I always love going there – the audience just seem to become part of things very quickly; it's almost like we merge together.

It was getting towards the end of the evening when I felt a man come through. It was an older man; a man who I sensed did not feel comfortable with himself. I explained: 'I have a man here who's really struggling to make a connection. An older man. He wants to but he feels a little hesitant. I don't think he's happy with himself. He is looking for some help and I'm hoping we can give it to him.

'Does anyone have a loved one who had an operation to have perhaps a liver or kidney removed?' I continued.

A lady in the fourth row put her hand up. 'Yes, my father had an operation,' she said hesitantly.

'I'm sensing he was a man who had trouble making his feelings known.'

'Yes,' she said quickly, pushing a strand of mousey hair behind one ear. 'He made life very hard for himself as well as others.'

'He wasn't there for you, was he?'

'No, he left us and then, when he remarried we lost contact for a long time.' A note of regret coloured her voice.

'He says he knows there are issues he should have resolved and that he wants to tell you that what he did was wrong,' I said. 'He has many, many regrets that he did not resolve these issues in his physical life.'

'Yes, I understand. I wish he hadn't left it but I'm glad he's saying it now.'

'Darling, I think it's very important that you can find it inside you to forgive him so he can feel at peace.'

'Yes, I agree. Thank you very much.' Her eyes shone with understanding.

Secret: we can still tell our loved ones how we feel about them from the afterlife.

Once we have forgiven ourselves and forgiven others for the hurts we have received from them, we will be in a much stronger position to take the next steps we need towards healing hurt and coping with our grief. And we can do this by letting go of the past and moving on to the future.

5 | Secrets of Letting Go and Moving On

You might be reading this book hoping for a revelation, or series of revelations that will shake your world and make you see everything in a new light. But who says our world has to be turned completely upside down in order for us to see things differently? The fact is that often the real secrets are lying right underneath our noses. But because we are caught up in the past, we don't understand them. A lot of the time we are focusing on those who've passed over when we should be thinking about ourselves. When a loved one dies, it can be tempting for those left behind to focus on the past and put their own lives on hold. Some people sink so low they are lost to themselves and the world for years. Others just need a few words of reassurance to come to terms with their loss and to start living again.

Some people have a feeling of guilt about, for instance, giving away closets full of clothes that someone else could make good use of, long after their initial grief has been put to rest. Other items that were the possessions of their loved one are dust collectors. Some feel moving on in their lives is wrong, even though the grieving has been laid to rest and they have accepted that their loved one is not coming back. Guilt causes them to feel they are being disloyal but this is just not so. What they are doing is simply continuing life as it should be done.

Learning to Grieve

Sometimes you notice people in the audience without actually looking for them. This time a tall, handsome woman caught my eye. It wasn't so much her physical presence as the look on her face that attracted my attention. She was anxious in that way that some kids are in school when they have the answer to a question. I later found out that she 'just knew' she was going to get a communication. She was with a man who looked very like her who I imagined must be her brother.

I stepped forward. 'I've got a connection with a lady here who is trying to show me that at the time of her passing, or leading up to her passing, she was incredibly frightened. And I feel that I want to connect to her daughter. She says she just held onto your hand and said, "Just hold me, hold my hand."'

The handsome woman put her hand up. 'I think it could be me.'

'Is that a family member with you, darling?' She nodded. 'What's your name?'

'Denise – and this is my brother Andy.'

I said, 'My love, it was you who held Mum's hand, and reassured her, "Don't worry, it'll be all right", wasn't it?'

Denise had that look of someone struggling to hold back the tears but she managed to murmur, 'Yes, it was me.'

'It was you; you held Mum's hand. And my love, if I get this wrong forgive me, but I feel that she spent quite a long time on a trolley.'

'She did. They were looking after her but it was very cold and sterile in the hospital. I know she was frightened, very frightened before she died, and I knew it was me just clinging onto her hand, holding it tightly.'

'She's just put in front of me three boxes, three quite big boxes. And she's saying it is time to pack everything away. All right? She feels as though it's time the three of you, her and you two here, should be strong enough to get three big boxes and just pack everything away. And she just wants it to happen. She's adamant that you will do it together…' I said firmly, then added, 'She enjoyed the garden, yes?'

Denise piped up: 'Well, she enjoyed sitting in the garden but not doing the work! Andy did all the work. We've put her ashes in the garden because we found out that she wanted to stay in the garden, and we've tried to make it as nice as possible with different kinds of plants. She just loved sitting in the garden.'

'Now, Denise and Andy, I want you to understand that it wasn't the thought of passing that bothered her, but she hated illness. OK?' I looked at them both and continued, 'She's saying, let's be grateful it was short, because I couldn't have coped with a long illness.' I paused, before asking, 'What am I getting the taste of Tia Maria for?'

Denise laughed. 'I would make Black Russians at Christmas, or if we went out somewhere.'

'She knows that before the year's out there's one more important event to come up,' I said.

'Yes, there's a big party coming up.' Denise was smiling but had tears in her eyes. Mixed feelings are not uncommon when people receive communications from those who have passed over.

'Just remember she will be there, and she's giving me the taste of Tia Maria and saying, "This was always the way it was finished off."'

'Yes,' said Andy.

I continued: 'Now it's time to pack everything away.'

'It's very hard to do, even though you know you should do it just in a practical sense. I mean, like any woman she had a lot of clothes, and I just felt that while the clothes were still there, she was still there.'

'That's perfectly understandable,' I agreed. 'But it's time now for you all to be strong enough to get three big boxes or as many as you need and just pack everything away.'

'Well, I suppose it's about moving on, isn't it?' said Denise. 'I mean, she probably wants me to move on. It's difficult when you lose someone you love, it is just so devastating.'

'We've all been there for each other,' said Andy. 'But we feel really lost sometimes. She is probably right to say move on. But you move on in your own time, when the grieving is perhaps coming to an end.'

United in their loss, Andy and Denise faced me bravely and I felt sure that those three boxes would soon be packed, and their mother's wishes fulfilled.

Thomas Edison and a New Start

I like this story about Thomas Edison because in many ways it reflects the truth that we can always start again, no matter how much has gone before.

It was a cold December night in West Orange, New Jersey. Thomas Edison's factory was humming with activity. Work was proceeding on a variety of fronts as the great inventor was trying to turn more of his dreams into practical realities. Edison's plant, made of concrete and steel, was deemed 'fireproof'. As you may have already guessed, it wasn't!

On that frigid night in 1914, the sky was lit up by a sensational blaze that had burst through the plant roof. Edison's twenty-four-year-old son, Charles, made a frenzied search for his famous inventor-father. When he finally found him, he was watching the fire, his white hair was blowing in the wind. His face was illuminated by the leaping flames.

'My heart ached for him,' said Charles. 'Here he was, sixty-seven years old, and everything he had worked for was going up in flames.

When he saw me, he shouted, 'Charles! Where's your mother?' When I told him I didn't know, he said, 'Find her! Bring her here! She'll never see anything like this as long as she lives.'

Next morning, Mr Edison looked at the ruins of his factory and said this of his loss: 'There's value in disaster. All our mistakes are burned up. Thank God, we can start anew.'

Secret: life does not stop when our loved ones pass over. After bereavement we must make the gradual effort to move on and move our lives forwards.

Sometimes we have to let go of people. It gets to a point where it's inescapable. During the course of my life I have had to cut myself off from people. I have done it because it felt to me that to go on seeing them – in whatever capacity – would not be right. Perhaps we were no longer on the same wavelength or had travelled in different directions. When I realised I had to make a break from them I did it because I took responsibility for myself and my own life.

Of course there were times when I felt bad about cutting my ties with other people but in the end we are all here to make the choices that are best for us. And we should not feel guilty or allow the other person to make us feel guilty if we do. However, our feelings about letting go of a relationship and moving on can become complicated by a number of factors, such as misguided loyalty and overwhelming guilt.

The unexpected loss of a loved one is one of life's hardest blows, as shock can become mixed up with grief in an overwhelming combination. But of all unexpected deaths, the suicide of a loved one must be one of the most difficult losses to cope with. Suicide often raises painful questions, including doubts and fears for those left behind. The survivors of suicide – the family and friends of a person who completes suicide – may ask themselves: Why wasn't my love enough to save this person? What could I have done? How did I fail? What will people think? At these times, feelings of failure, shame and blame heighten the sorrow of loss. Survivors may feel isolated and judged by society, friends and colleagues; in fact, some cultures see suicide as shameful or an affront to God, making the emotions of survivors a particularly complicated and painful burden to bear.

The Woman Who Ignored the Truth

One warm June day a young woman came to see me. As it was one of the first sunny days of the year I had a particular spring in my step. However, this contrasted sharply with my visitor, who moved as if she was pulling a truckload of bricks behind her. She was perhaps only in her late thirties but seemed a great deal older. This wasn't just because of superficial things about her such as the lines on her face: it was the whole way she carried herself. She had an air of weariness, of resignation and of having been dealt a rough hand by life. Well, that was how she appeared to me, anyway.

She accepted my offer of tea and so I invited her to sit down and relax while I nipped into the kitchen. The afternoon sun was streaming through the window to where she sat, but I could see her trying not to fidget as she waited for the sitting to begin.

It didn't take long before I felt the very intense and powerful presence of a man coming through. 'There is a man here who seems very determined to me. He is – how shall I say this – one of those people who loom large,' I said.

Her eyes widened. 'Yes, I know somebody like that,' she murmured.

'He doesn't seem to want to let go of you.'

She nodded and looked uncomfortable, nervously looking up and down and around the room.

I gave her a moment to compose herself before I continued, 'I'm being shown a violent death of some sort. It seems to me there was an early death and it was him.' I said that I felt he had taken his own life.

She went on to explain to me that the large man had been her partner. Things had not been good between them for a long time. She had known she couldn't continue living with him as it was making her desperately unhappy. The problem was that he wouldn't accept her decision. Every time she tried to tell him, he would threaten to take his life.

'I felt like I was being pushed and pulled all the time. It was no way to live. Finally I decided I had no choice but to go – so I did,' she confessed.

'And he committed suicide when you left ...'

'Yes. It was my fault.' She looked down at her hands in her lap.

I couldn't believe she'd actually said that. For one thing, it was very clear to me that this man had been totally in charge of everything he did. He had got his way throughout his life and now he still seemed to be doing it even though he'd passed over. This young woman couldn't see that if anyone could be described as a victim in their relationship, it was her. Yet here she was, still in his grip.

'It seems to me like he is still managing to make you feel guilty,' I explained.

She tilted her head to one side as if she was trying to avoid the issue and wriggled in her chair. It seemed I had hit a nerve.

I continued, 'He put all his problems on to you but he didn't bother trying to deal with them himself. I think this man is trying to make you feel guilty from beyond the grave.'

'No, I'm really fine,' she protested. 'I'm very positive now.'

It was the least convincing thing I had heard in a long time. I reached out and gently touched her arm. 'I think you might be saying that to yourself but I don't think you are positive at all, my love. I think you are carrying guilt on his behalf. And this guilt has nothing to do with you.'

She closed her eyes for a moment as though trying to shut the thought out, and then finally she appeared to acknowledge what I'd said: 'Yes, I suppose I am.'

'Darling,' I continued, 'you're sitting here, waiting for a message from a man who made your life hard, threatened to kill himself and then did so. He made those choices himself, without you. And now you're the one who's stuck and can't move forward. Do you see what I'm saying?'

'Yes, you're right Colin,' she sighed. 'But I can't seem to shake him off. It just seems like I'm carrying his problems around with me.'

'Why not give him a message? Tell him that you loved

him but now you've got to move on. It's your right to speak to him, you know,' I added.

She looked incredulous. 'I can do that?'

I explained, 'Of course you can, my love. You can tell him it's time to move on. I think perhaps that's why you have been given this opportunity to speak to him now.'

And in that room, with the afternoon light fading to a golden close, that's what she did. Finally this young woman, who had been living a life of guilt, realised that she had no reason to be burdened by regrets any more. She didn't have to wait for him to come to her to make her peace with him: she could go to him.

Secret: never be afraid to think and feel the truth about someone who has passed over.

It is never too late to let go and make a fresh start. But it is not always easy to make the transition, especially if our emotions have become complicated by outside factors and we feel as though we are responsible and guilty for the actions of others, or – at the other extreme – the victim of circumstances over which we have no control. Then life can seem unfair. This can be particularly true when we think about illness and death.

When we are well we may feel invincible and so there is nothing that can prepare us for the shock and devastation of a terminal diagnosis. The knowledge that we can no longer take our lives or the lives we share with our loved ones for granted takes away our ability to plan for the future and removes hope from our lives. When a loved one becomes terminally ill, we grieve in anticipation of their death, we grieve for the loss of them in our lives and we grieve for our own mortality. And rest assured, I've been through it just like you.

However, on this occasion the woman sitting with me thought she was the only person who'd been 'cheated' out of her life by death and could not accept that she could go on and maybe even form new relationships. I'm not suggesting that everyone who loses a spouse will want to create a new family environment after a certain amount of time has passed. There are those who are perfectly happy being on their own. Some find that they are alone, but do not feel lonely.

The Woman Who was Angry with Death

One wind-swept October day, I met a woman for a private sitting who seemed very angry from the word go. As she entered the house, a gust of wind and leaves followed her inside and I hastily shut the door behind her. Introductions and pleasantries aside, we sat down and began. Bizarrely I found myself seeing an impression of … a can of Heinz soup!

I said to her, 'Your husband wasn't English, was he?'

'Why do you say that?' she wondered.

'Well, I think he was foreign, maybe German.'

'Actually, yes, he was.' She nodded firmly.

'Was his name Heinz?'

'Yes.'

I continued: 'And did he wear that aftershave – what's it called – Eau Sauvage?'

She seemed a little bit shocked. 'My goodness, he wore it all the time!'

At that point, I could see the anger in her face; it was oozing out of her. In fact it went deeper than that: she was angry at death itself. Now, I know what it's like to lose loved ones and to watch death take them away before your very eyes, so I understand those initial feelings. The difference was that this woman had been angry for a long time. She appeared to have blocked the world out and, even though she had chosen to see me, she wasn't really listening to what I was saying.

So when she said to me, 'You don't understand, you haven't lost anybody,' it was clear she felt that death had dealt a personal blow to her. It was as if she'd been picked out from the crowd.

'I assure you madam, I have lost dear ones and I know how that felt to me,' I replied politely.

'I've had my husband taken from me,' she snapped. That word 'taken' was said so sharply. She really believed it. As we spoke, I discovered that her husband had had a brain tumour and had passed on at a relatively young age, before his fiftieth birthday in fact.

'Your husband is saying you should calm down and get on with your life,' I told her. 'He says he has nothing but happy memories of your time together but it's time for you to create some more of your own.'

She looked at me coldly and said, 'If I cannot have the man that I want, then I don't want anybody.'

Now I've sat with a lot of people who I've found uncompromising in some way – and understandably so – but this woman was being so unrealistic. She could not accept what had happened was now done and seemed to want some redress or retribution for her loss.

I repeated, 'It's clear he feels you should move on and wants you to do so with his blessing. You're still relatively young and may meet someone else.'

'I most certainly will not!' she snapped frostily. And that was that.

A few years later I bumped into her again at a golf charity dinner. She was totally changed, having met a man and remarried. There was an aura of ease about her, and she was about to take early retirement. Her previous attitude of 'How could you die, it's not fair!' had changed and now she was ready to accept and forgive.

 **Secret:** when a person passes over we should never despair of future happiness; otherwise we are insulting their memory and abandoning the greatest gift they gave us.

The wisdom of those who have passed over is something we all miss. Suddenly the person we relied on to guide us and help us make decisions is not there for us. One of the great challenges in society is that we are all of us conditioned to look for a leader. And that can be any sort of leader: religious, political, someone from our family, a teacher at school. These are the people whom we look to make our decisions for us. And sometimes when we get used to people making decisions for us – such as our partners – we confuse this with our love for them. But that's not love. That's dependence.

Whilst we all have to be dependent on others to some extent this shouldn't mean that we can't function without them. This is why although I'm dependent on my friends I can also make up my own mind without them. All the same, if they're not around I sometimes find myself thinking, 'What would this person think of this?' I find I also do that with loved ones who have passed over. I often think of Michael, who was like a big brother to me. It's been quite a few years now since he passed over but every day I can feel his presence just as strongly. Sometimes when I'm struggling with a decision I'll think, 'Now, Michael would probably say I should do it this way,' and I find the thought gives me great comfort and reassurance. He may not be here physically but what I learned from him won't ever die.

A Grandmother's Wisdom

People often think that just because someone they loved and respected has passed over, their loved one knows far more than the person themselves. This is not always true.

Often they are telling you what you already know, simply reinforcing your knowledge for you.

Standing in front of a packed auditorium in the north of England, I suddenly felt the presence of an older woman come through. She definitely had something she needed to say and there was a sense of urgency about her. I sensed she was a formidable character and she was insistent that I find the right person.

'Does anyone know Annie?' I wondered.

As there often is with large audiences, there was a long pause. Even if people do know somebody, they can take a while to register the fact in this sort of environment, as the circumstances can feel a bit overwhelming. I looked around and continued: 'I'm seeing a woman with lots of children and I'm thinking they might be grandchildren.'

A lady in a pink blouse put her hand up. 'My grand-mother was called Annie,' she said; it was a bit difficult to hear her at first as she was very softly spoken.

'Darling, she has a very definite message for you that she seems anxious to pass on,' I said firmly.

The lady nodded. 'I think I might know what it is.'

I smiled. 'She's saying that you need to be what you really want to be. Stop listening to everyone else telling you what to do. Go and live your life the way you want to live it. Does that sound like something you might expect to hear?'

The lady in pink nodded vigorously and I could see she suddenly had a new energy, almost a sparkle, about her. 'I've just left my husband after sixteen years!' she announced. 'I always put him first. In fact I've always put other people first. And now I've realised that I've been cheating myself out of life.'

'So you're finally looking after yourself?' I asked.

'Absolutely,' she declared. 'At long last, I'm being who I want to be. Life is far too short.'

'And that was what your grandmother told you before she died.'

'She was always looking out for me – I was her favourite – this is exactly what I needed to hear.'

The lady in pink had always known what she had to do but hearing her grandmother's words that night made her feel even stronger and determined to take action.

 Secret: those who have passed over still feel the same way about us. Those feelings do not stop just because they are not here in physical form.

When we're caught in the devastating grips of significant loss such as death of a loved one, it's difficult to believe that we have enough inner strength to cope with what is being asked of us. The process of learning to cope after a death can take months or even years and some people feel like they never truly recover from the death of a loved one.

I know it might sound almost glib to say this but, believe me, everything in life has a purpose. The wide range of emotions that we as human beings experience each have their place. Living and dying have purpose also. Death is not some random event that picks out certain people: it comes to all of us! That's why understanding the true nature of life and death can help us live our lives with energy, joy and hope. As you move on and look back you'll be able to focus less on the sadness and more on the happy memories, which is exactly how those who have passed over would want it to be.

Just because people have passed over it doesn't mean we have to forget them. It won't be physically the same but they are still with us and so are the things we learned from them. When someone passes over, they are still with us and so is their knowledge and comprehension of our lives. Thus their communication with us is part of our lives, even though they may not be with us in a physical sense.

Pickled Onions and Cabbage

It was a Saturday night in Oxford a few years ago. We'd arrived for the show earlier that day and I had spent a lovely afternoon wandering through the old university colleges with their magical dreaming spires. At times I found myself standing there wondering just what secrets these buildings were keeping. The fresh air had done me good and I felt invigorated for the evening's show.

The first communication came through. 'OK, I'm up here on the top row; I've got to come right to the end because I know I want to be near the ladies in black, with the gentleman and a lady up there,' I said as I focused on the audience. 'Is there a connection between you two, because the energy seems to be settling in and around both of you? I've got a gentleman with me and I'm hearing Country and Western music,' I added.

'Yes,' said one of the women, smiling.

'What's your name, darling? Valerie? Yes? OK. Bless his little cotton socks, he's got a terrible voice because I can hear him singing "Ruby, don't take your love to town". 'Cos he did quite like Kenny Rogers, didn't he?'

She gave a little laugh. 'He certainly did, Colin! My husband was a very fun-loving family man. As you said, he loved Country and Western music. He had this huge collection of records and would play them day and night. Dolly Parton was his favourite, but Kenny Rogers sang a lot of Dolly Parton songs too so he liked that.'

'But why is he showing me a trumpet or a bugle?'

'I'm not sure about that; I don't think he owned one,' she said.

'My love, if you have a look back and talk to some of the older members of the family, someone will have memories of him trying to play a bugle.'

'He was always doing it, puffing with his mouth. You know how some people pretend to play musical instruments. It was quite funny actually.'

'OK, that must have been because there was a time in years gone back when he tried to play a bugle. I can hear that kind of trumpeting sound.' (After the show Valerie phoned her brother-in-law and it turned out that he had been in the Cadets with her husband, where they had both played the bugle.)

'He was always humming,' said Valerie. 'It drove people mad sometimes. He'd do it everywhere. In the queue at the bank for instance.'

I focused on the man next to her who, it turned out, was Valerie's son Richard, and I confirmed that he had children of his own.

'Yes, I have one son – Daniel.'

'All right, now, what have you taken away from your boy that you won't let him play with? Because if I'm getting this right, I feel this is Dad who's trying to connect with me.'

'My dad?'

'It's definitely a father figure. He wants to know what you have taken away from his grandson.'

'I take a hundred things away from my son every day.'

'No, this was yesterday. You took something away from him and said, "You're not playing with that!"'

Richard thought for a moment, then replied, 'That might have been a pen.'

'So it was up the stairs – the paint or the writing – on the skirting board?'

'There's a piece of skirting board that we haven't stuck properly yet and much to my annoyance he keeps picking that up.'

'Well, after what he did to the skirting board, I'm not surprised that you don't want him to have the pen. Your dad loved his grandchildren. He's concentrating on his wife now, and there's something about losing front teeth.'

'He did,' said Valerie.

'Yes, because he's showing me all the front teeth missing – I don't know why it's so funny, but there's something funny about it, because I can hear him laughing away as he's talking about it. So what is it about the front teeth?' I wanted to know.

'He just had two little fangs here, and he used to always laugh and say he looked like Dracula.'

'And who had to keep the large jar of pickled onions?' I asked her next.

'I did,' said Valerie.

At this point the audience giggled. I understood: sometimes communications can be so mundane and everyday it makes them even more surreal.

'There always had to be a large jar of pickled onions,' she told me. 'I used to have to pickle my own.'

'But not that red cabbage stuff.'

'No, he liked red cabbage,' Valerie said firmly.

'Oh, I know what he's on about now; if we went home and opened the cupboards there would be a jar of picked onions but no red cabbage!'

'Yes, that's right.'

'Apart from that, he's telling me there's not a lot of things that have changed; there's the same old routines, and you do things as if he was still here.'

'Yes, well we're trying to. It helps us.' Valerie looked a little sad.

'You don't have to, but he knows why you do,' I explained. 'Not so long ago, you even ironed a shirt of his. Yes? You can understand that? The way he's putting this through to me is that you were half way through ironing it before it occurred to you that he wasn't going to wear it. But can you tell us why you were ironing it?'

Valerie dabbed at a tear in the corner of her eye. 'I started to iron it,' she said, 'and then I just stopped and put it back in a black sack that I was putting his clothes in for charity, but yes I did start. I suppose I thought it would bring some sort of normal routine. I was feeling lost but getting this message has helped me a great deal.'

Her husband wanted to offer her some words of comfort: 'Your husband is saying it will die down and it will get better. He leaves his love with you.' Valerie and Richard looked at each other and smiled.

Secret: it's fine to feel displaced after a loved one dies but to be mindful to concentrate on healing yourself, since they are at peace already.

When someone passes over, the members of that person's family can either retreat into themselves or seek out one another. For some people grief is intensely personal and that's fine for a time. However, inevitably there are responsibilities to be gotten on with and people to take care of. What I can say is that in all my years of speaking to souls in the spirit world I rarely get a sense of sadness in their communications since they have accepted what has happened, which is exactly what they want us to do too.

Many times the general message is 'just get on with taking care of business'. This can be difficult but all I can say is that if you accept death is a continuum of our physical life, then perhaps you can understand why you should carry on.

The death of someone we love can conjure up all sorts of emotions we never thought existed. This energy – for that is what it is – must not be swept under the carpet but all too often it is. The attitude to death in Western societies, of not discussing it until it actually happens, only serves to make us fear our own deaths even more. As a result we are unable to help those who are bereaved or grieving. It is fine to grieve but at some point we have to ask ourselves, 'What would my loved one think of this?' My work over the years has illustrated to me that our loved ones do not expect us to grieve indefinitely for them. Nor do they expect us to tiptoe around the subject of their death and not talk about it. By the way, don't think that just because I communicate with the afterlife, I find the death of my loved ones any easier. Like you I feel the pain of loss. But I know they are with me and the best thing I can do is include them in my discussions and in my life through my behaviour.

Talking about the Dead

I was in Birmingham doing a show. I've mentioned Birmingham before: the city is one of our most popular locations where tickets tend to sell out very quickly. The audiences there are also very good and very supportive.

I was getting the feeling of someone trying desperately to connect. They seemed to be struggling to breathe and I was sensing lung problems. I explained, adding, 'I can say for sure this is an elderly gentleman and there is the letter "P".'

A woman wearing a bright red dress put her hand up. 'One of my grandparents had lung cancer,' she explained.

'Was it your grandfather?'

'Yes. He died of lung cancer when I was about eighteen; I can clearly remember him getting cancer and going downhill very, very quickly with it. My grandad's name was Percy. He worked for the coal industry; however he worked on the admin side, not in the mines.'

'My love, what's your name?'

'Louise.'

'Louise, I have to ask you – what is your connection with children?'

'Well, I have two lovely children of my own ...' Louise looked a bit blank.

'No, no,' I persisted. 'It feels like there's something far more substantial than that. What is your connection to children who have passed over?'

Louise opened her mouth to answer and then seemed to hesitate. 'My sister gave birth prematurely to a baby girl, who passed.'

That still wasn't the full picture. 'I'm absolutely sure there is still more to this,' I said. 'There must be more than one. Do you understand about five children that passed into the spirit?'

'Yes Colin, I can.' Her lips trembled slightly but she looked me straight in the eyes.

'Right. Well, I think this is Grandad's way of letting you know that all five children that have passed to the spirit are safe with him there.'

After the show and away from the audience, Louise told me that she was very surprised I'd managed to get the actual number of children correct. The family had been dogged by deaths of children during pregnancy. It seems that two of her sisters lost children when they were twenty-two weeks pregnant. They both gave birth to them, named them and had funerals for them, but the babies were stillborn. Another of Elise's sisters had tragically suffered two miscarriages. The first of these was twins and her second miscarriage occurred only eighteen months later.

I continued with the communication. 'Louise, either yourself or one of your sisters will have a strong fascination with the word "Ellie" or "Ella". If it doesn't make sense to you, talk to your sisters and find out what is the thing with this name "Ellie" or "Ella".'

Louise later said that she did indeed speak to both of her sisters about the name Ellie and it turned out one of them was fascinated with it. It was her preferred name for a girl, which was most appropriate since she was apparently pregnant again and things were going well for her this time.

'Grandad knows you've been talking a great deal about your mum recently with one of your sisters. Is that correct?'

'Yes, it's absolutely right,' Louise confirmed.

'I can't feel if she is still here or has passed so I'm going to have to ask, is Mum here or is she in spirit?'

'She's passed.'

I focused again. 'OK, she passed some time ago but she has become a big topic of conversation recently, though for a long time you didn't speak about her.'

'I haven't been able to talk comfortably about my mum since her death twenty-five years ago,' Louise confided. 'I know my sisters talk about her quite a lot, and they talk to my dad about her, but I came to this reading hoping she would come through. I suppose I wanted to talk about her and needed some sort of sign.'

As we talked, I discovered that Louise's mother's name was Diana; she had died of motor neurone disease when Louise was just fourteen. Louise had had no idea how ill her mother was until she died and had been away on a school trip at the time, which made it even harder for her. Louise said sadly: 'I missed the last few days of her life. I think this is part of the reason I haven't been able to talk about her, even to my sisters, and I just wanted some message from her to know that she was still there in spirit and she was watching over me and the children, and that she's just there for us.'

'My love, I really do feel that Grandad is trying to get some connection from your mum through to me, but I don't know if he is going to be entirely successful. I feel as though he will have to talk for her, rather than actually connect her, and he is trying.' I continued: 'When each of you married, there was something that connected each sister to your mum. She's putting it through in a very odd way: "There was something of me with each of you." I think it's her way of letting you know that she was there with everyone in spirit.'

'It might be that all three of us wore a piece of jewellery at our weddings that had belonged to Mum,' said Louise, adding, 'There are certain times in your life when you really wish your mum was there with you, and knowing that she was there in spirit is absolutely great.'

Later, Louise told me that she felt lighter in some way after the message. 'It's so good to know that my mum and grandparents are still there with me. I find it such a comfort and I know now that I will find it a lot easier to talk both to my mum and about her to my sister, which will help me with the grieving process.'

She was also happy to be able to pass the message to her sisters that her grandfather is there with them and all five babies were together. She felt that, after such tragic pregnancies, it would help her accept what had happened and be able to grieve and move on.

Secret: it is healthy and necessary to come to terms with our feelings about death.

As I've mentioned before, there are times when I meet people who I feel are profoundly spiritual; I come away from meeting them feeling much richer for the experience.

For all of their suffering, they seem to have obtained a view of life that puts everything into perspective somehow. That isn't to say that their grief is any less real, just that they seem to be able to find a place for it in their lives that enables them to move onwards, rather than stay trapped in the past.

A Man without Bitterness

The interaction between this life and the afterlife was very much on Andrew's mind when I met him at a social event. I instantly liked him; he had a kindness in his eyes and a firm handshake. We got talking and I could tell that he was a thoughtful, considerate man who was given to reflection. When he discovered what I did for a living he took me to one side so that we could have a conversation without being overhead. We found two chairs in a corner and, as the chatter flowed in the room around us, Andrew quietly explained that he was in his late forties and that he had once lived happily with his wife and two sons in Lincolnshire. But they had been killed in a tragic car accident and now he wondered if I could help him connect with them.

Andrew told me he remembered the day of the car accident very clearly. However, like many others who have lost loved ones suddenly and tragically, he felt displaced by the speed of their departure into the spirit world. In many ways that was the aspect that was troubling him the most. Astonishing as it may sound, I think he'd accepted their deaths; he just couldn't accept the rapid nature of his family's passing.

Despite the hustle and bustle around us I focused and found the connection I was seeking. Then I told him the truth straightaway: 'I'm not sure at all if your family all passed over at the same time.'

He nodded in understanding.

'When the delivery van hit your car, there was no time. But there is something else ...'

'Go on,' Andrew urged me, his eyes shining.

'What I'm feeling from this communication is that you all passed over – all four of you. And it appears that one of you was put back because someone had to come back to the physical world.'

Andrew admitted that he thought his time had come in the accident. 'You know that light at the end of the tunnel stuff?' he began, but stopped, as though searching for words to explain what he had experienced.

'Yes,' I said gently.

'I remember seeing it and I remember all of us rubbing our heads ... well that's what I thought I saw.'

Andrew was interesting to me because he didn't ask why he came back. Once again, it was as if he automatically understood the big picture. In talking to me, he seemed to be looking for some confirmation that everything was as it should be in the grand scheme of things.

Drawing on the link I had with his family in the afterlife, I could offer him the reassurance he was after: 'Your wife and sons are at peace and want you to know that. They are with you, in a different state of existence and they understand that you're still with them and are connected to them.'

Andrew's reaction was one of relief. He was a very deep and wise man; here was an individual who carried no bitterness in circumstances that would have made most of us bitter for the rest of our lives. Instead, Andrew focused on the positive things about his family and what they meant to him, not just in the past but in the future as well. He chose to create his own reality out of what could have easily been a very negative situation.

Secret: the afterlife teaches us that we can choose how we wish to view death, and that even tragic loss may be part of a greater pattern.

Accepting that a loved one has gone is never easy. On losing someone close, there may be a tendency for some of us to think, 'They are no longer in my life. I have all this pain and hurt because of that so I will avoid their memories in whatever way I can.' This is perfectly understandable in the first instance. But usually when people begin to adjust to their loss they begin to realise that the person who is no longer there physically is nevertheless still with them and so is everything they shared.

When my friend Michael died it was devastating. As I have mentioned before, Michael helped me find my way in the world, advising and encouraging me. When he died I initially found life meaningless but after some time I realised that I could make his death meaningful. In fact it was his passing that inspired me to concentrate on my mediumship full time.

Picking Up and Carrying On

I stood in the theatre feeling a very powerful connection coming through. Somebody had obviously liked Doris Day. I looked round the audience. 'Who liked Doris Day?' I wondered.

A man in his fifties put up his hand. 'What's your name, sir?'

'Ted,' he replied, before adding, 'My wife liked Doris Day.'

'"Que Sera, Sera"' – that was the one she liked, wasn't it, Ted?'

'Yes, I think so, yes, I didn't mind it at all either.' Ted gave a little smile.

'I get the feeling that she must've really quite liked that tune at the time when it first came out.'

'I would've thought she did,' Ted agreed.

'She's giving me the thought or memory here of something to do with freshly baked bread or a connection to a bakery.'

Ted nodded. 'She loved freshly baked bread.'

'OK, because the communication is so incredibly strong I can almost smell it.' I could too – and it was delicious. 'I'm getting a name that begins with 'M' – Mary, no, Marion,' I said.

Ted explained, 'My wife's name was Marion, and we were married for thirty-seven, nearly thirty-eight years. She was everything to me and although she's passed over, I know she hasn't gone permanently. She had a great sense of humour and she found lots of things hilarious. She could be very serious as well, but in general she was just wonderful – that's all I can say.'

'Ted, listen to me.' I walked over to him. 'She needs you to know that she has met up with someone and now I'm getting the initial 'M' again. Ah, OK – your mother's also spirit-side and your wife used to call her Mum. That's right, isn't it?'

'Yes, she did, yeah.'

'OK, I know what she's on about: she needs you to know she's with your mum.'

'My mother, her name was Angie,' Ted said. 'She was very sweet but you were in trouble if you got on the wrong side of her! Fortunately her and Marion got on like a house on fire.'

Marion was trying to tell me something, but the details weren't all that clear: 'Ted, what have you put in the garden for your wife's sake? She's saying, "There's something in the garden for my sake."'

'Oh!' Ted's face registered surprise. It's not uncommon for people, halfway through a communication to suddenly realise 'Oh goodness, this is really happening'. He cleared his throat and said, 'A neighbour gave us a small rose bush in a pot.'

'And there is something either near or around it which is either stone or concrete?'

'Yes, it's on a square slab in a pot.'

'She's telling me you don't like going to the cemetery. Can you understand that?'

'Yes.' Ted bowed his head for a moment.

'There's no need to – there's absolutely no need – because she knows you have an issue about it. She also knows you're feeling bad about it. I'll tell him, darling: she's not there.'

'I'm realising that.' But he still wouldn't meet my eyes.

I looked at Ted, feeling for this gruff man as he struggled with his loss. Marion repeated the message and I passed it on: "There's no need to go, because none of us are there, I'm not there,' she said. 'There's no reason for you to.'"

'A-ha,' said Ted, realisation dawning. 'This comes not solely from Marion but also my parents. I used to go to visit their graves and she used to come with me, but every time I came away from there I was physically sick. As far as Marion goes, she was cremated and I do go to visit the cemetery, but not as often as I should. I've had a lot of guilty feelings about that. She was right in what she said – that I do feel guilty so it's good to know I don't have to feel like that anymore. Hopefully after this I won't.'

'She's saying, "It's time to go to our place again." There is one particular hotel or B&B you used to go to.'

'Yes, yes there's a little place…' Ted smiled wistfully.

'It seems that since your wife's passing you haven't been back there.'

Ted shook his head. 'No, I haven't because they're no longer open.'

But with Marion's prompting, I knew there was more to

it than that: 'You've pretty much avoided the area, haven't you?'

'Certainly have,' Ted agreed.

'It's time to go back.'

'I'll try. I really will.'

'You've done a pretty good job, Ted, recovering from your wife's passing. Don't be too hard on yourself.... She's showing me and she's saying to you, Ted, there's still one part of you that just won't live. She promises she won't leave you. Listen to your son when he talks about doing the trip that you and Marion planned. Do it.'

Ted looked teary but sounded determined: 'I'll try.'

'She'll be with you. She's promised she'll never leave you.'

Ted had got caught up in thinking that he'd lost Marion forever. While of course he could not be with her physically, that did not mean he had to forget or try and wipe out their happy memories.

Secret: our loved ones are peaceful and happy and they want us to know happiness too.

Two Travelling Angels

Two travelling angels stopped to spend the night in the home of a wealthy family.

The family was rude and refused to let the angels stay in the mansion's guest room. Instead the angels were given a small space in the cold basement.

As they made their bed on the hard floor, the older angel saw a hole in the wall and repaired it.

When the younger angel asked why, the older angel replied, 'Things aren't always what they seem.'

The next night the pair came to rest at the house of a very poor but very hospitable farmer and his wife. After sharing what little food they had, the couple let the angels sleep in their bed where they could have a good night's rest.

When the sun came up the next morning the angels found the farmer and his wife in tears. Their only cow, whose milk had been their sole income, lay dead in the field.

The younger angel was infuriated and accused the older angel, 'How could you have let this happen? The first man had everything, yet you helped him. The second family had little but was willing to share everything, and yet you let the cow die.'

'Things aren't always what they seem,' the older angel replied.

'When we stayed in the basement of the mansion, I noticed there was gold stored in that hole in the wall. Since the owner was so obsessed with greed and unwilling to share his good fortune, I sealed the wall so he wouldn't find it.'

'Then last night as we slept in the farmer's bed, the angel of death came for his wife. I gave him the cow instead. Things aren't always what they seem.'

Sometimes that is exactly what happens when things don't turn out the way they should. If you have faith, you just need to trust that every outcome is always to your advantage. You might not know it until some time later...

Looking Forward to Living

William Lawrence returned for one of our special *6ixth Sense* shows in which we revisit a reading to find out what has happened since we last met the person involved. I'm always curious to see how the person has fared since I last met them and what, if any, impact the reading had on their life.

William was a retired ambulance man who told me he enjoyed doing crosswords. He seemed to be trying to keep himself busy, which I felt was a good sign. 'I'm working on a project, building a huge model of the *Titanic* and I love it!' he announced. At the same time he said there were certain things he'd like to know: 'I would really like to know if there is life hereafter.'

When I first met William, I had discovered that his wife was spirit side and she'd come through to say that she was happy for him to get on with his life. She'd also asked about some legs being taken off a bed! (As I've said previously, spirits will often talk about mundane things to identify themselves.) As soon as William heard the words 'bed legs' he knew it was her. 'This is something only my wife and I knew about. I hadn't mentioned it to my family or any of my friends, so, it must have come from the spirit,' he told me. William explained that he and his wife had moved to London into a tiny bed-sit. Their rickety bed had only two good legs on it, as the other two were propped up with books.

Then, one night his wife had gone to sleep in a hospital bed and not woken up.

William gazed thoughtfully ahead. 'From what I heard, she was taken to hospital and she had a sudden collapse,' he said.

I'd told William that his wife was telling me she'd had a seizure. She wanted him to know there had been no great suffering there. He looked relieved when he heard that.

I continued: 'She says, "It was just like going to sleep and waking up in another state of existence." She seems to have this feeling that you've always been concerned about the fact that you weren't there.'

'Yes,' William said quietly.

'She also says it doesn't matter. When you actually went to the hospital it seemed that everything was conspiring against you in your attempts to get to her. Does that make sense to you?'

'Yes, it does,' William confirmed.

'It seems to me there were an awful lot of things getting in your way and delaying you.'

William nodded.

When we met for the second time, William explained, 'My wife suffered from a condition called lupus, which attacks the whole body. Even though I knew that my wife was going to die, when it actually happened I was completely devastated. I thought that I was going to go first.'

I thought back to our earlier meeting: 'Yes, that's what your wife came through and said at the time. Her exact words were: "How wrong could you be? How totally wrong!"'

William continued, 'It got to be a standing joke with us actually. I was hoping to go first; I didn't like the idea of being on my own, I think perhaps I was being a little bit of a coward...'

Another interesting thing that came out at the reading was William's desire to go to see the Taj Mahal in India. He told me that since his wife's death the proposed trip didn't feel right and he'd been umming and aahing about it. The message had come through from her that he should do it as she would be with him on his travels. As a result when we saw him this second time he'd made plans to go away and was looking forward to his new adventures.

 **Secret:** those we have lost want us to carry on living our lives, making plans and having adventures. They will always be there to watch over us as we continue on our way.

People often ask me if it's easy for me to stay connected to those who have passed over in my life. Obviously they assume that since I'm a spiritual medium it should come naturally. Well, no, it doesn't. It requires dedication and thought; perhaps not in the same way that you work to stay connected to your friends who are with you in the physical life, but nonetheless you still need to apply yourself. And, as I frequently point out, a spirit will only come through when they feel the time is right.

Nonetheless I feel we can all stay connected, no matter in what circumstances our loved ones passed to the spirit world.

At the same time it's easy to feel life stops when someone passes. But is that what they would want? Remember, even though they are not with us physically, we still have a two-way relationship. They would not want us to give up our lives for them. In fact if we do that then we're saying we have given up hope. In my view it is an insult to that person's memory and to the gifts they gave us in order to live our lives. If we accept that life and death are part of the same picture, then we should follow our desired path.

Not Forgetting the Living

We were in an auditorium. It was an older one in a seaside town, a bit musty but elegant and grand in its own faded way. With its deep red walls and curved ceilings it created quite an atmosphere.

Standing in the centre of the stage that evening, I was getting what can only be described as a mum coming through. This was definitely a nurturing figure.

I spoke up. 'I'm seeing the letter A, possibly Alice. Does anyone have a mum by that name who's in spirit?'

'It could be me.' A pretty blonde woman with a sunny disposition put her hand up.

'Darling, I'd like you to step forward so we can make this connection a little bit stronger. That's right. Down the front. Can we make some room? Thank you.' I turned back to her. 'What's your name, my love?'

'Gillian.' She giggled a little.

'Gillian. And Alice is your mother?'

'Yes.'

'Gillian, Alice is telling me that she wasn't ready to go but she wants you to know that she's fine. She's happy with her situation and accepts that it had to happen for a reason.' Gillian nodded. I went on: 'She's also talking about travel.'

'Oh –' Gillian half-turned towards the row she had come from in the audience. 'My husband wants to work and travel abroad.'

'So I'm right in saying he was thinking about it when Mum was still this side of life?'

'Yes, very much so.'

'Well, we all have our choices to make. As human beings we all have free will to make our own decisions.' I paused. 'Now I'm getting the impression that your mum knew about this.'

'Yes, she did,' Gillian confirmed.

'So you'll understand when she says you need to think very seriously about it now?'

'Well, I think so…' Gillian looked at me, her head to one side.

'Now, I believe that for some time after Mum passed you carried something around in your bag that belonged to her. Some texture, perhaps a cloth.'

Gillian nodded firmly. 'Yes, it was a handkerchief.'

'Right. She also knows that you never said goodbye and she wants to tell you she's still with you and that she is close by.'

It became clear that Gillian's mother had collapsed at a family party. One moment she was smiling happily and full of life, and the next she suddenly fell to the floor. She lost consciousness and never regained it. A few days later she died.

'It was such an emotional occasion,' said Gillian, 'and I just don't think we ever expected that death would occur so suddenly. She'd had such a happy time and enjoyed her life and her job. She worked in a clothing shop and all the customers adored her. Her social life was always full and interesting.'

'And this trip abroad you wanted to take, why didn't you do it?'

'My husband has had a dream of doing something totally life-changing and he wanted to go to America and start a new life. I wasn't totally against it but I was worried because since my dad passed I never really wanted to go and leave Mum.'

'She knew what you wanted, my love,' I assured her. 'I think she knew you wanted it even more than you did. She's saying that you should not feel guilty and you must do what you want now.'

'Yes, I realise we've put things on hold. I need to talk to my husband about things now.'

'And remember, Gillian – you're not saying goodbye to her,' I concluded. 'We never have to say goodbye as long as we believe. We can still carry on our lives and be close to those who have passed.'

Gillian's smile lit up that faded theatre.

Secret: we need not put our lives on hold because loved ones have passed over. We will do more justice to the memory of those who have passed over if we live our own lives to the full.

So many secrets from the afterlife are about the qualities that will help us to move forwards here on the earthly plain. They are about love, about friendship, hope, spirit and forgiveness. They are about creating new futures for ourselves in which our loved ones who have passed still have a place, watching over us and guiding us as we carry on with our life's journey.

Conclusion

We arrive on earth as spiritual beings in physical bodies. As we grow from being babies to children, especially in Western societies, we come to believe that spirituality resides outside us. Little wonder that at times our lives seem so difficult, often unnecessarily, and everything appears to be a struggle. So we start to look for answers which for an increasing number of people means searching far and wide. There is nothing wrong with looking for answers but in many cases the answers are right in front of us.

That's where I feel that the afterlife can help us. Our loved ones who've passed over are already people we know and trust. Their passing gives them the additional benefit of being able to see the big picture and thus they are in a position to give us the guidance that we may be looking for. The spirit voice is not necessarily about huge revelations. Often it just exists to remind us that we need to listen more, to tune in to ourselves. We might find creative inspiration, love otherwise lost, a renewed desire to forgive. We may find the basis for a major life transformation. Whatever you're looking for, I hope you find it in the secrets in these pages.